MAVIS BLACKMORE
£27 860167

THE BONUS OF LAUGHTER

THE BONUS OF LAUGHTER

An Autobiography

Leslie Crowther
and Jean Crowther

Hodder & Stoughton

First published in 1994 by Hodder and Stoughton
A division of Hodder Headline PLC

British Library Cataloguing in Publication Data

A CIP catalogue data for this title is
available from the British Library

ISBN 0 340 62468 X

Typeset by Hewer Text Composition Services, Edinburgh
Printed and bound in Great Britain by
Mackays of Chatham, Chatham, Kent

Hodder and Stoughton
A division of Hodder Headline PLC
338 Euston Road
London NW1 3BH

PHOTOGRAPH CREDITS

Leslie and Jean Crowther, BBC Copyright Photographs, Bristol
United Press Ltd, Roy Keirby/North Thames Gas Board, Sidney
W Baynton, Middlesex County Press, Houston Rogers, Daily
Express, Granada Television, Mirror Group Newspapers, Thames
Television, Eastern Daily Express, John Alexander.

Contents

Acknowledgements

My thanks go to Florence (Jean) Nightingale, without whose love and devoted nursing I wouldn't be here now.

To my neighbourly amanuensis whose wordprocessing skills and typist's fingers have enabled this book to come into existence.

And finally, to Hodder & Stoughton's own Rowena Webb without whose whip, constantly applied, this manuscript would never have been completed.

Foreword

I can't recall what I was about when President Kennedy was shot, but I do remember what I was doing when my wife Sue came to tell me that Leslie Crowther had been involved in a serious accident.

I was in the garden, near the narrow road leading to Leslie's house, from where so often during our years as neighbours I had returned his cheery wave from the passing Rolls. But now – for how long? – there would be no Rolls, and no Leslie. The one was lying a crumpled wreck by the side of the M5; the other was fighting for his life in Frenchay Hospital, Bristol.

The Rolls is still absent but a year or so after his accident, as I write this, Leslie is very much with us. By *us* I mean the village, which has had a proprietorial interest in him since he and his wife Jean set up house here fifteen years or so ago and which has ever since been warmed by his geniality, has basked in his reflected glory and enjoyed the friendly generosity of both.

I use *us* also in the sense of the wider world from which he was so precipitately withdrawn on that October day in 1992, but to which he is returning with increasing vigour. His visit to Lords during the 1993 Test series and attendance at Buckingham Palace to be invested with the CBE (Crowther's Bloody Effort) were evidence of his return to this wider world, giving assurance of a recovery which to his thousands of well-wishers has seemed little short of miraculous. Indeed it is, as those of us who live nearby can attest.

Our village has a lively church, a thriving junior Sunday Club, an active village hall committee, and sports and recreation facilities which are the envy of surrounding communities. It was in All Saints on the Monday following the accident weekend that many of us gathered – a spontaneous coming together. Richard Hall, our rector, was there but there were no formal prayers. Instead each of us silently made our own, or numbly tried to come to grips with the probability that Leslie would die, or at least be permanently brain-damaged – this was the tone of the hospital bulletins.

Looking towards the pew where Jean and Leslie usually sat, I found it impossible to imagine a family service without the distinctive chuckle which would encourage the children in their enactment of some biblical scene, or the drama he could impart to the most prosaic Lesson for the Day. Jean, of course, was at that moment by his side in Frenchay, where she or other members of the family were to remain until he came off the critical list. They also were remembered.

The strength of the prayers and hopes for his recovery flowing upwards that day were such as to put in peril the church roof – recently repaired at a cost of some £65,000, raised through a year's events including a one-man show given by Leslie before a capacity audience in the nearby parish hall.

And it began to work. As the days became weeks, the bulletins from the intensive therapy unit gave increasing cause for hope. We had to keep at it, though, and only when we saw Jean smiling again did we know that between us – surgeons, hospital staff, family, villagers and, of course, Leslie himself, we'd pulled it off.

No banners were displayed in the village on the day in February when he came home. Everyone realised that the road to full recovery would be a long one. Nevertheless, as he began to get out and about, the rapidity of his progress along that road was a delight to us all.

One day, almost a year after the accident, I was weeding the rockery near the drive, feeling pretty good because I'd just finished reading the page proofs of a book I'd written. I looked up and saw him walking down the drive towards me, debonair in blazer and Lord's Taverners tie, and I suddenly thought: 'Why don't I suggest . . . Why doesn't he write . . .?

2

Why don't I ring Jean . . .?' So I did and he has – or rather, they have, for no one but Jean could have told the inside story of the months following the accident.

So this is it, in their own write. My humble part as Leslie's amanuensis (a word that both of us had to look up before committing it to print) has been, during the course of many conversations, to draw out his reminiscences, get him to write them down, and dash back to my word processor – though after a while it was more a matter of keeping up than drawing out.

I think it's been a kind of therapy for him. I know it's been one of my most enjoyable experiences, and I suspect that Jean and Sue have found that, for the time it has occupied us, we have both been even easier to live with than usual!

Graham Harrison

To Leslie with my love and thanks

Part One

Jean's Story

The Accident

The present that our son Nicholas gave Leslie for Christmas 1992 was a watercolour he had painted, entitled *The Autumn that You Missed*. It had been a beautiful autumn, full of reds and golds, though in early October there had been a patch of very wet and windy weather. And it was like that on Saturday 3 October as Leslie drove back home along the M5 after opening the new Allied Carpet Stores in Birmingham.

I had been worried about him when he left on the Friday to go to a Lord's Taverners dinner at Swansea, after which he was driving to a Birmingham hotel. As President of the Lord's Taverners he had had an extremely busy few months, and I knew he was very, very tired. I had been sharing the driving to many of the venues, but on that Friday I didn't go with him as my mother had died two days before. We were all feeling very sad: though she was ninety and had been declining rapidly since suffering a stroke six months before, she was an amazing lady. I am one of a large, devoted family, and Leslie and she were particularly close. My eldest sister Pat and her husband Ken had come over from France, where they live, for the funeral of Ken's mother who had died the previous week, and they had stayed on at our house near Bath for Mummy's funeral. My younger brother was flying over from Canada with his wife, and my other sisters and brother were all arriving at different times.

We had made all the arrangements for the funeral, which was to take place on Tuesday, 6 October. On Saturday morning, after we had cleared Mummy's things from St Teresa's nursing home in the village, Richard Hall, our rector, called to see Pat and me. Lunch was late, and afterwards I started to make a

9

large batch of spaghetti sauce to serve on Monday. At about 3.15 the telephone rang and I took it in the hall.

'Is that Mrs Crowther?' It was a man's voice.

'Yes.'

'Mrs Jean Crowther?'

I don't know why, but at this point a slight stab of fear went through me. I sat down. 'Yes,' I replied again.

'It's the motorway police, Mrs Crowther. Your husband has been involved in an accident on the M5, near Junction 10.'

'Is he all right?' I asked as calmly as possible.

'He's conscious and gave us your telephone number. They've just got him into an ambulance and are taking him to Cheltenham Hospital. I'll give you their number, but I suggest you wait about twenty minutes before ringing.'

My heart was pounding as I went back into the kitchen.

'Leslie's had an accident,' I said to my sister, and repeated the gist of the message. Then I got on with the spaghetti sauce, thankful for something to do. But the twenty minutes seemed an age.

The hospital answered promptly when I rang and quickly put me through to the Accident Department, who told me that Leslie had just arrived. They hadn't yet fully examined him, but he'd been able to tell them all the tablets he was on for his heart condition. They suggested I come at once, bringing him an overnight bag.

'Tell him I love him,' I said.

'He sends his love to you,' the nurse replied.

A strange calm comes over you at a time like this. Automatically I packed a bag with his things. Pat insisted that Ken should go with me but just as we were about to leave Charlotte, our youngest daughter, walked in with her children Alex and Clemmie, four and two respectively.

'I'm coming with you,' she said on hearing the news. 'D'you mind having the children, Tante P?' Pat, who had been a Norland nanny, agreed at once.

We drove to Cheltenham without a lot of chatter. I stopped to fill up with petrol – which was fortuitous. I remember saying as we approached the town: 'Oh God, I want to be there – and yet I don't.' My stomach was churning.

10

When we arrived at about half past five we found the Accident Unit strangely quiet. A pretty blonde sister met us and took us straightaway to see Leslie. The young woman doctor with him explained that he had lapsed into unconsciousness, but that this was not unusual after a head injury.

Leslie had a bad injury around his left temple which was coated with blood, but apart from that he was unmarked. I went over to kiss him, but at that moment he suddenly began to choke, whereupon in a scene reminiscent of *Casualty* the cubicle suddenly filled with flying figures. Charlotte and I were shown into a small waiting room and told that the consultant would be coming to see us. He explained that the X-rays had revealed a cracked neck bone. As yet there was nothing to panic about, but after a blow such as Leslie had sustained they would be watching him closely. He suggested I stay the night in Cheltenham, and advised me to inform all the family. It was now just after six and he was going home, but he said he would return at about nine to check.

For the next half hour we were busy ringing round the family. Amazingly for a Saturday night they were all in, and we promised to keep them posted. But soon after we had put the phone down on the last call things began to take a turn for the worse. When the consultant walked in again at about 6.45 I knew something was wrong. He told me he wasn't at all happy about Leslie's condition and had ordered a brain scan.

It was then that two kind and sympathetic officers from the motorway police arrived, bringing Leslie's overnight things and the other contents of the car in large plastic bags, together with a brown envelope containing Leslie's watch and keys. I asked about the accident, and only then learned that the car had turned over and over and mounted the verge before coming to rest upside down. I thanked God that no other cars had been involved.

By then the press had also arrived. Apparently they listen in to the police radio bands, and it was in this way that they had got wind of the accident. Fortunately the reporters had been intercepted by a hospital administrator, who had put them in another waiting room and locked the door!

Just after 7.15 we were told the true gravity of the situation:

11

to have any chance of survival Leslie had to undergo major brain surgery, and arrangements were being made for him to be transferred immediately by ambulance to the renowned neuro-surgery unit at Frenchay Hospital in Bristol. A police escort was being laid on.

Quietly the consultant advised me to get all the family to Frenchay as soon as possible. I rang home first and spoke to Adam, Charlotte's husband. I wanted him to ring Richard Hall, our dear rector, to ask him to pray for Leslie. The rest of the family were told, and all said they would get there. Charlotte, with me in Cheltenham was distraught – but, strangely enough, comforting her helped me immensely. I knew I had to remain calm, load the car and line it up behind the ambulance ready to trail it to Bristol.

I drove well that night. I have a great faith and certainly I was given extra strength to help me. The police were absolutely marvellous. 'Stay behind the ambulance all the time,' they told me. 'We may be behind you at times or in front of the ambulance, but you just remain in position.'

The slip-road to the motorway was coned off. They let us through and then closed it again, and on we sped through the night. I followed those blue flashing lights for an hour and a half, praying all the way. We were in the middle lane with the police car behind in the outside lane. It felt like being under the protection of a shepherd. Only once did the ambulance slow down for a while, and I remember saying to Charley: 'I think he's gone.' Other than that, no word was spoken.

I can't describe my feeling of relief at seeing the signs for Frenchay Hospital. Off the motorway and through the red lights we went, then up to the hospital's Accident and Emergency entrance.

The next few hours are still rather a blur. Caroline, our third daughter, with Charlotte's husband Adam, had arrived as Leslie was being taken out of the ambulance. They joined us in a small waiting room and we held each other as the tears flowed.

In another small room adjoining the Acute Ward we met David Sandeman, the neuro-surgeon, who was quickly to become 'our hero'. He explained the operation he would be carrying out and was absolutely honest about the gravity of the situation, which was not improved by Leslie's existing heart condition. If he survived surgery he would be transferred to the Intensive Therapy Unit. The ITU waiting room was full – they had had a busy day – but we moved down there as soon as it was clear.

The operation started at about 9.45. Some time after ten our daughter Liz arrived, driven from London by an actress friend. Then came Nick, with Claire, his wife, whose mother had taken charge of Leah, their baby daughter. Caroline's husband David arrived next, and last of all came Lindsay and Peter, who live in Hastings and have twin boys aged three and two daughters. They too had been driven by a kind friend.

It was almost 1.30 a.m. before David Sandeman came to see us. He told us that Leslie had almost died during the operation, but they had got him to ITU and now all we could do was wait. The next forty-eight hours would be critical – every minute he survived would count. I asked if I could see Leslie and he said we could go in two at a time, briefly – Leslie was still being worked on.

This was my first experience of an ITU – a sort of cocoon to which you gain admittance by pressing an answercall button in the corridor outside and identifying yourself. Nick came in with me, and after we had sprayed our hands with blue disinfectant we walked over to Leslie's bed at the end of the ward. There he lay, head bandaged, body attached to a life support machine with tubes everywhere, a small white sheet covering the lower part of his body. Nick held me while I cried. The pain of grief is hard to bear.

We stayed a little while, and then the rest of the family followed in pairs. After our return to the waiting room a nurse brought blankets and pillows. The room was small and we were rather a crowd, so some dozed in a waiting room opposite which was blessed with a coffee machine that the computer-literate younger folk managed to operate.

I couldn't sleep, and I remember going out into the small courtyard behind the waiting room which seemed to be in the throes of renovation. The rain had stopped and the sky was clear with stars. Suddenly a generator started up, making me

13

jump. 'Oh God, I don't believe this is happening,' I said aloud.
But it was.

Hours passed, during which we went in and out of the ITU.
Then early on Sunday morning someone told me that there
was a room available in the bungalow provided by the WRVS
(Women's Royal Voluntary Service) for patients' relatives.
Knowing that my vigil would be a long one I decided to
drive home, collect some night clothes and washing things and
prepare to camp out at Frenchay indefinitely.

At home the phone was ringing incessantly. My poor younger
brother and his wife had arrived early at Gatwick from Canada
and seen the headlines about Leslie's accident, so they were
shocked as well as jet-lagged. Dear Pat, as always a tower of
strength, was cooking dinner and holding the fort.

I remember going upstairs, standing on the big landing of
our lovely house and thinking how pointless and useless it all
seemed – possessions meant nothing. Trying to lie down was
impossible: each time I closed my eyes those blue flashing
ambulance lights took over as if imprinted on my brain.

By now, of course, the papers and TV were in full cry and
I realised that both the family and the hospital were going to
need some help in dealing with the problem. The new Director
of the Lord's Taverners, Patrick Shervington, and his wife,
Vicki, lived near us in Bath and I rang him when I got back
to the hospital. Patrick is an ex-army colonel with tremendous
organising abilities whom we had got to know well – and to
appreciate – during Leslie's second year as President of the
Taverners. He came straight over to Frenchay and immediately
sized up the situation.

I think it was difficult for members of the family to have
someone they didn't know introduced to the scene, and I could
understand their reaction. On the other hand we needed help.
Our first priority as a family was to concentrate all our time,
love and effort on the task of bringing Leslie back to life.

Calling Patrick in turned out to be a godsend, and we
shall never be able to repay him for what he did – nor
the Taverners for their support. In liaison with the hospital
administrator, arrangements were made for coping with the
press and public who were jamming the switchboards. From the

Monday following the accident the Lord's Taverners mounted a telephone service to receive calls from public, press and others anxious to wish Leslie well and ask after his progress. This took an enormous load off our minds. We were not only relieved at being able to concentrate on Leslie, but we also knew that the great tide of good will flooding in was being dealt with sympathetically.

All day Sunday we took it in turns to sit beside Leslie. He looked very noble and still. The nurses asked what they should call him and we told them simply: 'Les' (this had all begun when he became 'Les the Pres', as the Taverners had dubbed him). So each time they prepared to turn him or attend to a line or drip they would offer a gentle explanation to 'Les'. The physiotherapists who also came in every few hours to help patients with their breathing followed suit.

On Sunday afternoon I took my things to the WRVS bungalow, which became our sanctuary for the next three weeks. There were two bedrooms, each with two beds. We had one room, and the other was occupied by another family. There were also a sitting room with a TV, a fridge, facilities for making hot drinks, and a bathroom with a shower. We were in touch with the outside world via a payphone, and with the ITU by direct link. Everyone's heart missed a beat when the latter rang!

For the first week one of the family shared the bedroom with me – taking it in turns since they, of course, had their own lives and families to cope with. Between us we maintained the vigil at Leslie's bedside. I couldn't sleep. I would try to do so around ten o'clock, but would usually be back in the unit by about 1.30 a.m. One night later on, when I returned at 2 a.m., a voice over the entryphone said: 'You're late. Have you brought a note?!'

On Monday, 6 October I had to go early to Keynsham near Bristol to deal with some business about Mother's estate – to add to everything, Leslie and I were her executors. On my way I had to pass St John the Baptist's church, where we had been married thirty-eight years before. I went in and knelt to pray, then sat there sobbing for a while. A kind lady broke off from arranging the flowers and came over to console me – just one instance of the overwhelming kindness we experienced during this crisis in our lives and which helped to see us through it.

I needed all the help available on my return to Frenchay with Lindsay, for after negotiating the encampment of journalists I found that the news was gloomier than ever. The nurse on duty had felt unhappy with Leslie's condition, and at her suggestion another brain scan had been carried out. This had revealed another clot that had formed, so he had to go back to the theatre.

This time the operation took two and a half hours, and once again David Sandeman took time to explain the surgical procedures to us and to give his assessment of the prospects. These were not good. With complete frankness he told us that the situation was grim, and that in his opinion Leslie had less than a fifty-fifty chance of recovery.

Sensing the crisis, the press had become desperate for inside information. As a precaution two security men had been placed outside the ITU, and the corridor had been screened off as they took Leslie to and from the theatre. For the other families with loved ones inside the unit this must have been an added strain. Their worries and fears were as great as ours, and they really must have wondered what all this madness was about. At a time like this the outside world becomes extremely remote and all your concentration and energy are taken up within those four walls. But there was great understanding on the part of the others keeping vigil. The empathy which built up within the unit was amazing: over the weeks we would all rejoice if a loved one made great strides towards recovery, or mourn with the less fortunate, knowing full well that we might have to face a similar outcome.

My mother's funeral was by now looming large. I had intended to drive myself home on the Tuesday morning, attend the service at twelve noon at All Saints, Corston, followed by cremation, and then return immediately to Leslie's bedside. Caroline's husband, David had organised caterers to cope with those coming back to the house afterwards, and the rest of the family had rallied round to make sure that the arrangements were complete.

During Monday night, however, I realised that I couldn't

16

face the thought of driving myself, so at 7 a.m. on Tuesday I telephoned Patrick to ask for his help. He came to collect me, bless him, and drove me the dozen or so miles to home in good time for a clean-up and change.

The sight that met me on my arrival was overwhelming. The whole of the terrace was covered in baskets and buckets of flowers which seemed to have cascaded from the house, where the downstairs was a sea of colour – all sent by dear friends, fans and organisations of every kind, including the Prime Minister and Mrs Major.

The funeral was extraordinary in the way that it acted as a catharsis for me. The hymns we had chosen were poignantly apt, especially the first, 'Fight the Good Fight', which had us all in tears. It was followed by 'Oh Lord and Father of Mankind, Forgive Our Foolish Ways' and finally 'Lord of all Hopefulness, Lord of All Joy'. Nicholas bravely took over the reading his father would have done, and did it magnificently. The first was Henry Holland's 'Death Is Nothing at All', followed by a short piece entitled 'Stephen's Poem' which I had found on a news cutting tucked in Mummy's wallet.

> To all my loved ones –
> Forgive me and forgive those that trespass against me
> Do not stand at my grave and weep
> I am not there: I do not sleep
> I am the thousand winds that blow
> I am diamond glints on snow
> I am sunlight on ripened grain
> I am gentle autumnal rain
> When you waken in the morning hush
> I am the soft uplifting rush of quiet birds in circled flight
> I am the bright stars that shine at night
> Do not stand at my grave and cry
> I am not there – I did not die.

I shall never forget Nicholas reading that poem. During the service in that packed church, surrounded by such a wonderful family, with friends, nuns and staff of St Teresa's and the villagers – just like an extension of the family – I suddenly

17

knew that I had to hand Leslie over to God. There was really nothing I could do, and whatever the outcome might be I had to accept it. It was an oddly calming feeling, and after Mummy's cremation I returned to the hospital to resume the waiting.

Our rector, Richard Hall, who had given such a lovely address for Mummy, came to the ITU to pray with me. By this time Leslie's head was very swollen and he really looked dreadful – I could read the shock on Richard's face, though he tried hard to disguise it.

Afterwards, in the waiting room, I said to him, weeping: 'Oh, Richard, what am I to do? I don't think I can face another funeral – it will be mayhem.' The press had even been in the bushes at the crematorium with cameras.

Bless him, he made no attempt to dismiss that thought. 'It will be, Jean,' he replied, 'but we'll manage if we have to.' I thank Richard for that honesty.

Later on the Tuesday following the accident a small glimmer of light shone amongst the gloom and I witnessed another example of the help and kindness of the motorway police. At some time during the previous two days I had gone through the brown envelope given to me in Cheltenham to retrieve Leslie's house keys, which I wanted to hand over to Nicholas. But they were missing and, though Nick searched through all the other bags we had dumped in the garage at home, he couldn't find them. This was a great worry, as among the keys were those that worked our burglar alarm system. Where could they be? Suddenly it came to me – before starting a journey Leslie would always take from his pocket whatever keys he would need on arrival and drop them into the tapes compartment between the front seats in the Rolls. Assuming he had done this on Saturday, it was more than likely that they would be where the car had overturned.

Patrick duly rang the Cheltenham police, who replied simply: 'Leave it to us' – no mention of needles or haystacks. Their sang-froid was justified since they went to the spot where the car had landed on its roof and, by a miracle, found them embedded in the mud. The key-ring carried a photo of Leslie and the initials L.C., so it would have been easily identified had it landed in the wrong hands.

18

Wednesday, 7 October was a glorious autumn day, but unfortunately for us the news was not so good. David Sandeman called us together and told us that, although Leslie had started to come round, this had brought on some fits – a not unusual development following brain surgery. Because of this he would be administering a heavy-duty drug which would put Leslie into a deep sleep and at the same time control the convulsions.

My poor husband! Yet another machine was connected to him – this time to measure the electrical impulses in the brain. By now he was looking very swollen; Caro thought he resembled a cabbage-patch doll, though my image of him was more decadent – a bunch of grapes, I thought, and he'd have been the spitting image of Nero!

We were told that there was no chance of Leslie coming round for the next few days, so all we could do was wait. At this stage the whole family was depressed and tense. Although we were still taking it in turns to sit beside him he was too far away to be aware of us.

By now we had started to find our way around the hospital and grounds – the outside world seemed very remote. Frenchay is a beautiful village to the north of Bristol city centre near the junction of the M4 and M32. The hospital, set in its own grounds on what had been a grand estate, was built in 1943 as an American army hospital and the old part still retains a military camp appearance – blocks of buildings with long corridors, wards and theatres striking off at right-angles. Many of the entrances had thick plastic sheets instead of doors to ease the movement of beds and of trolleys carrying medical equipment. Over the next two weeks, as the weather grew frosty, dry leaves would blow into the buildings at night, and the walk from bungalow to ITU in the small hours was an eerie experience. I could feel the ghosts of servicemen and almost hear the stamp of army boots.

Mail had started to arrive by the sackful – it was really staggering. I had never before realised that Leslie was something of a national institution! Cards, letters, prayers, cassettes and drawings flowed in, all bearing kind and lovely sentiments. I think every school that Leslie had ever visited since *Crackerjack* days wrote in. Our local church school at Saltford sent a book made up of messages from all of the children. One little poem was so lovely that I wrote it out and stuck it with Blu-tak on to one of the machines above Leslie's bed. It said:

> Round the world and on the moon,
> Everyone whispers 'Get well soon.'

I read every card and letter and wept over many. We kept them all for Leslie to see, but it was to be many months before he could do so and even then he couldn't really take in so many thousands of them.

In ITU it is not possible to fill up space with either cards or flowers. Like the post, the latter were arriving in such profusion that Interflora rang to ask if they could stagger delivery over the next week. Liz took some of them to other wards, and we filled the bungalow and ITU waiting room too. We also found a ward that was saving postage stamps to fund a new piece of equipment, so we filled several carrier bags for them. Opening the mail, sorting it into piles and tearing off the stamps was a therapeutic exercise. The family members in the waiting room occupied themselves with that, helped by others who were also keeping vigil there.

Each evening, too, pages of telephone messages were faxed through from the Lord's Taverners with loving messages from the girls in the office, who were cheerfully coping with them all. It was totally impossible to answer all the goodwill messages, but I did get a note off to everyone who wrote sharing similar experiences of coma and ITU – they were immensely helpful and, even more important, hearteningly hopeful. At the end of the second week I sent a message to the Press Association:

> On behalf of the Crowther family I would like to thank everyone who has written to us or sent flowers over the past anxious days. We have been overwhelmed by hundreds of messages – prayers, cards, letters and tapes that have poured into Frenchay Hospital. Each one has been read and the love and kindness in them has helped us immeasurably. We are hoping to be able to read them to Leslie at some time in the future.

That love and kindness was reflected, too, in all the hospital staff, from post room right up to the consultants. It was marvellous.

Gradually now I was getting into some sort of routine. Early each morning I would shower and be over at the canteen by seven, when it opened. After tea and toast I would take a quick walk in the grounds before returning to ITU.

On Friday morning it was decided that, as the fits had ceased, Leslie could be taken off the heavy anti-convulsant. We were warned that the drug would take at least forty-eight hours to wear off.

On Sunday morning I went to chapel. As the organist played 'Jesu, Joy of Man's Desiring' I dissolved into tears and wept throughout the service.

Monday, 12 October is ringed round in my diary as Black Monday. David Sandeman saw us early and was very gloomy about the prognosis. He said that Leslie's responses were very poor, and for the first time it hit me that there might be a time when we would have to make a decision about whether or not the life support machine should be turned off. The family were all at a very low ebb and very scratchy with one another. I found myself speaking of Leslie in the past tense, and was rightly challenged by the others. My own feelings at that time were very negative. I knew how exhausted he had been before the accident and really wondered if he had the will and strength to come back.

That evening I told everyone that I wanted to be on my own, and sent them home. Returning to the bungalow, I had a loud, noisy cry. I really had reached rock bottom. I was worried about the family, too – if anything it was even more difficult for them. They all had their own families, jobs and homes to cope with, and Caro was in the early stages of pregnancy. Then I dried my tears, returned to my vigil in ITU, where, as always, the staff lent a sympathetic ear. They suggested I take a temazepam tablet to help me get some sleep. It was sound advice: I managed four hours uninterrupted and woke feeling more refreshed.

On Tuesday morning David Sandeman saw a flicker and asked a colleague who was doing brain research to carry out some tests. These took place between two and four o'clock that afternoon and the result was heartening. The brain stem seemed to be all right and the messages were getting through.

From that moment my feelings changed – now they were positive: we could all set to work and try to get through to Leslie. I found no difficulty in chatting to him. Liz brought in a Walkman and we started to play him tapes, both music and conversation. Don Maclean had sent me a copy of the interview which Leslie had recorded with him two months previously for Don's Sunday morning Radio 2 show, covering his childhood, career and honesty in facing alcoholism, so we used that. We also played Chopin's Fantasie Impromptu, which Leslie had used in his act.

Poor man! We bombarded him with sound. The village bellringers had made a tape of the All Saints peal – a sound that Leslie loved to hear coming across the meadows on Friday nights when they were practising. I remember telling him that I'd play them really loudly if he didn't wake up soon. Liz suggested that we talk to him in French so that he would be bilingual when he came round! As always, laughter helped to ease the tension.

By Wednesday I felt sure we were getting some response. He seemed to blink when I asked him a question, so I suggested he do it once for yes, twice for no, which he began to do. His eyes opened a little, too, though they seemed sightless. Amazingly, his glasses had survived the crash intact, so on Thursday they were brought in.

Though Leslie's left hand had moved a little there was still no response when he was asked to squeeze a hand. Charlotte brought the children in on Thursday afternoon and sat with Leslie while Alex, Clemmie and I went into the grounds and kicked our way through piles of autumn leaves – the colours were glorious. Clemency had her second birthday on Friday the 16th and it had been Natasha's (Caro's three-year-old) the day before, so on Friday afternoon, while more electro-physiological tests were being done, we had a birthday party at home. Claire, who had brought baby Leah down after Mummy's funeral, did most of the preparations. It was just the family and we did our best to give the little ones

22

a good time, but I found it quite difficult and returned to the hospital at 5.30 p.m.

On Sunday Patrick came in early to join me at chapel. Before we went in we visited the ITU and I asked him to tell Leslie to squeeze my hand. His military tones rang out, and it worked – there was a definite pressure, which was repeated on the next stentorian order.

We had a breakthrough! It was the right moment to go off to chapel. I knew from the mail that prayers were being said for Leslie all over the country, and it looked as if they were being answered.

It had been a long two weeks. When one of the doctors asked me how I was feeling I replied: 'Like one of the graphs on Leslie's monitor – up one minute and down the next!' He suggested that I start sleeping at home some of the time. I knew he was right – I'd been trying to avoid the outside world, but had to face up to it sooner or later, so Liz and I agreed to take it in turns to sleep at the hospital the following week.

On the Monday afternoon I went home and planted up the front borders with bulbs and wallflowers. I love gardening and it was a good thing to do – but all the time I was wondering if Leslie would ever see them.

Slowly the implications of a serious head injury were filtering through to me, both from the hospital staff and from outside sources. Among the latter was Headway House, a support group for patients with head injuries and their relatives. Rita Rees, the indefatigable founder of Headway's south-west area, rang me to offer support and sent over several of their publications which I found explicit and helpful.

By coincidence we had met Rita on Bath Station a few weeks earlier. Recognising Leslie, she had introduced herself, told him about their work, and asked him to visit Headway House at Frenchay. 'Of course I will,' he said, produced his diary and agreed to go on 16 September, just two weeks before his accident. He did, and came home very moved by what he had seen.

Leslie's injury was to his left temple. Although the workings of the brain are still something of a mystery, it is known that certain areas are responsible for speech whilst others affect

23

movement, vision, memory and personality. We laughed when David Sandeman mentioned 'personality' – I think I said, 'Well, a few changes there might be helpful.'

It was evidently good news that Leslie had been conscious and able to communicate immediately after the crash, but because of the two haemorrhages it was still difficult to know just how much he would be affected. There appeared to be no movement at all down his right side and I was warned that he might not walk again, or that if he did it could be with a limp.

The good news was that Leslie was left-handed. I remember saying to David Sandeman: 'Don't underestimate this man – he's pretty unusual.' I was thinking back to January 1990, when Leslie had spent forty-eight hours in the recovery unit at Bath Clinic following an emergency operation for a strangulated hernia. His heart had been a problem then, and I was staying at the clinic. When I went in to sit with him as he was coming round the sister said: 'Guess what he asked for?'

Warily I answered: 'I don't know.'

'The *Independent* crossword,' came the reply.

Leslie and I have done this together daily for years – even ringing each other to check progress when we are apart. On that day I went over to his bedside and picked up the paper, and sure enough two clues had been filled in with a wobbly hand. 'Hello, my darling,' I said. 'D'you need some help?' He nodded, and over the next three hours we completed it.

But whilst on that occasion he was out of recovery in forty-eight hours and home in five days, this time we'd be lucky if it was five months.

Still, he was improving, and over the next few days a decision was made to get him to start breathing for himself. He was still on the ventilator, so there would be no danger if he forgot – which he did quite often, making it bleep alarmingly. As he was gradually weaned off the machine the effort of having to breathe by himself was obviously tiring, but it certainly seemed to revive him. I found, too, that I could always get him to open his eyes by massaging his feet and toes, a practice which led to quite a few ribald remarks about certain members of Parliament!

By Tuesday, 20 October, when Leslie actually smiled, David Sandeman was feeling much happier about his progress. He was even prepared to make a statement to that effect to the press, who were still voracious for news and becoming more and more of a pain to all the family. The statement still had to be guarded, of course, if only to counteract the notion which many people still have that when you come round from a coma you just open your eyes, say 'Where am I?' and are restored to your former self. Would that it were so!

That morning I had gone to ITU early, as usual, and found the physios busy with Leslie. 'Give us five minutes,' they said over the entryphone, so I went into the empty waiting room. Just then the door opened and a young woman came in – she wasn't a member of any of the other families whom we had got to know, but I thought she might have been a new patient's relative.

'You're Mrs Crowther, aren't you?' she said.

'Are you a reporter?' I asked. 'If so, you're not allowed in here.'

'This is a waiting room,' she replied.

With the anger rising in me, I got up and left the room, saying that I was going to fetch the hospital manager. I didn't, but rushed into the loo opposite and burst into tears – I couldn't believe her insensitivity.

She had left the waiting room when I returned, but hovered like a vulture for the next two days, watching us all as we went in and out of ITU or spoke on the entryphone. It made me very wary when people came up to offer sympathy, and I hated feeling suspicious of everyone.

At an earlier stage in ITU Leslie had undergone a tracheostomy, and by the end of that week when he was doing all his own breathing an oxygen mask was put in place to assist the ventilation. He seemed to be getting a lot of fluid in his lungs so long suction tubes were inserted to 'hoover' this out, causing him to jerk alarmingly – something I found hard to watch. On Sunday, 25 October ITU was very busy, so Leslie was moved to one of the small side rooms on Ward 2. I found it quite daunting to be with him alone after the constant attention he had received in the Unit, though the nurses were always on

25

hand when the bleep gave warning that another 'hoover' was needed.

The first forty-eight hours out of ITU he found very exhausting and as his oxygen levels kept dropping he was moved back into the Unit on Tuesday the 27th, though I was assured that this was just to give him some rest. Indeed it did, and he slept for the next two days.

There had been a press report that Leslie had left ITU and on the Wednesday morning at about 9.30, as I parked at the hospital, a man with a camera got out of a nearby car. 'Can I have a photo, Mrs Crowther?' he asked.

'I'm sorry,' I replied, 'I really don't want one taken now,' and walked into the building.

Later in the day when it had got dark I went outside and was astonished when the same man jumped out of his car and started taking flash pictures one after another. It was crazy and frightening – I found I couldn't drive off, but sat there with my head in my hands and my heart pounding. When he eventually stopped I ran back into ITU. He did eventually get a shot with a telephoto lens as I left the canteen the next day. They don't give up!

Leslie woke the following night and made signs that he wanted to write. Pen and paper were provided and, although the result was almost incomprehensible, the nurses worked out that he was hungry so they tried him with a spoonful of yoghurt. He was dreadfully thin and very, very weak, but by the next day was ready to return to his room in Ward 2. So we said our farewells and thanks to the marvellous, never-to-be-forgotten staff in ITU, and Leslie moved on to the next stage of his recovery.

Fighting Back

It was now the beginning of November and Leslie had been in Frenchay for five weeks. During the next fortnight he remained very ill, developing a chest infection and requiring constant 'hoovering out'. He was put on to antibiotics and slept for most of the time.

I occupied myself for the first few days in brightening up his room. At last the cards could go up! I got special permission to use Blu-tak and soon three of the walls were covered with cards. Across the fourth, opposite Leslie's bed, I looped strings and hung up lots of the pictures sent in by schoolchildren and Brownie packs.

I knew we were in for a long, slow climb, and at this moment I was grateful for the fact that Leslie was a recovering alcoholic. When he had first made contact with Clouds House, the treatment centre he attended, I was told about the Family Programme which they run for the partners, relatives and friends of alcoholics. Alcoholism is an illness which affects the whole family: you know it's there, but try to deny it. My five-day course was a revelation. Previously I had often said that I had a headful of junk; this was my first opportunity to clear some of it out and look honestly at myself. Afterwards I joined Al-Anon, run on the same lines as AA but for family members. Their philosophies helped me all through these days. At the end of the Family Programme I had written myself a note, the last line of which read: 'Where there is fear, put trust.'

Many of my lowest moments following Leslie's accident were spent in the hospital chapel just sitting and reflecting. One afternoon, there came to my mind a story that one of our neighbours had told me. He is about our age and had been one of eight children. His mother, a devout Christian, had always gone to the Bible in times of stress and swore that the answer to any problem would be revealed in its pages.

One snowy day during his youth she had taken all eight children out snowballing and on her return found she had lost both her wedding and engagement rings. 'Right, children,' she said. 'We are all going to kneel down and pray, and then we'll go back and search in the snow.'

They did this and sure enough found one ring, though not the other. It was then getting dark, so she took them all home. 'I'll see what it says in the Bible,' she said, and opened it at random. Psalm 77, verse 8 met her gaze: 'Clean gone for ever.' 'That's it!' she said, closing the Good Book. 'We'll forget about the other ring.'

In front of me as I recalled this anecdote was a Bible, which I now picked up. It too opened at a Psalm: Psalm 13; 'How long Oh Lord'. Then my eyes alighted on the fifth verse: 'But for my part I trust in Thy true love.' There was no point in worrying about the future – it was enough to get through each day as it came.

After two weeks on Ward 2 Leslie still looked frail and weak and was quite unable to move himself around the bed. We take all our movements so much for granted and forget that everything we do is triggered by a message from the brain. One of the staff gave me an excellent analogy: 'Imagine Leslie's brain as a filing cabinet that has been upset and the files put back in a jumble. Most of the information is probably still there, but it has to be put back into the right compartments.'

His head, now unbandaged, revealed new stubbly hair growing on the left side, which had been shaved for the operation. The longer hair on the right side was combed over the growing hair in a Robert Robinson-type slick. It was still tinted with what we irreverently used to call the 'Sheep Dip', and the whole effect was somewhat bizarre!

During those early weeks of November we started to get to know all the staff on Ward 2. It was then that the physiotherapists (or physio-terrorists as Leslie later dubbed them) Chris and Sian came on the scene, followed closely by occupational therapist Nicki and speech therapists Rachel and Jacqui. Leslie presented them with quite a challenge. One of the major problems in ITU had been getting the balance of medication right for his heart condition as well as for the brain injury. But slowly and surely, as if by magic, the combined efforts of doctors, surgeons, nurses, therapists and dieticians began to work.

Chris and Sian started by getting Leslie into a sitting position with his legs down over the side of the bed. This could only be done with Sian kneeling on the bed, supporting him from behind. Even so he looked like a rag doll, with his head lolling forward.

On 12 November they decided to try him on a tilt bed, used to restore equilibrium after a patient has been lying prone for a lengthy period. Chris told Leslie to raise a thumb whenever he felt dizzy. He was obviously apprehensive about it, but they won his implicit trust by their gentle manner of introducing it to him and gradually, with a few stops on the way, they got him upright. I remember thinking how tall he looked. They tried it again next day – Friday the 13th but even on that inauspicious day they succeeded and he remained upright for a little longer. That day he seemed more awake and alert than he had been before.

Because Leslie had been on a life support machine his swallowing reflex had been affected, which meant that he had to be fed by a tube inserted through his nose. I was aware that he hated this, and it became patently clear to everyone else when he pulled the tube out. Over the weekend of 14–15 November he removed four in succession! They were difficult to put back and so the nurses reluctantly decided to immobilise his left hand, tying it to the side rails of the bed. The right hand remained free as it had little discernible movement. I went off to lunch in the canteen and on my return was confronted by a nose tube dangling over the rails on the right-hand side of the bed. Leslie was sleeping peacefully: the determined – and successful – effort to remove the tube with his right arm had obviously exhausted him.

Later that day I told David Sandeman of my concern that Leslie was feeling fed-up and frustrated, and that if we didn't get him going soon he might give up. David passed on my feelings to the others, and on the Monday the physios got him out of bed and into a large chair. He sat there like an old man, sagging over to the right, but managed to endure it for twenty minutes before indicating that he would like to get back into bed. But it had worked! I could see now that the fight was there. By the end of the week he was starting to hold his head up well on his own, though his back still needed some support. The swallowing reflex still wasn't working, but he accepted that the tubes would be removed as soon as it was safe to do so – that great day came on 30 November.

Then work began on his speech. The tracheostomy still prevented him from speaking but Rachel and Jacqui, the speech therapists, got answers to their questions by holding up cards on which were written three words, and getting him to point out the correct one. In this way they were able to assess his understanding and memory, both commonly affected by head injuries. He coped remarkably well, though his reactions were noticeably slow and his attention span limited. Everything had to be done in short bursts, as he quickly became exhausted.

It was obvious that he had a compulsion to write, and his continuing efforts to do so were meeting with some success. Sometimes he would write backwards, as a child does, though more often the letters would start off medium size and soon become smaller and smaller. It was all done at great speed and it was difficult to slow him down. By the third week in November it had improved a lot – he could write his name well and was able to write brief answers to questions I asked.

Rachel had suggested I bring in photographs of the family and get Leslie to identify people and places. This I did and it worked well. One morning he had been sitting in his chair for about ten minutes, identifying grandchildren – most of them correctly – in photographs that I was showing him. Then I held up a picture of Lindsay's daughters. 'Who are they, Les?' I asked.

He wrote down: 'Sarah and Leila.'

'No, Les,' I said. 'That's Sara and Kristina.' Very deliberately he crossed out the 'h' of Sarah and then wrote '*Bollocks*!'

'OK, Les,' I said. 'I've got the message – you've done enough.' He grinned.

The occupational therapist, Nicki, was the one who got Leslie's hand and arm working so well again. It took a long time and it was marvellous to see how patiently she went over and over the smallest movements, gradually getting some life back, first into the fingers and then into the whole hand.

By the end of November it was suggested that I bring in a tracksuit and some T-shirts so that Leslie could get dressed in the mornings. Nicki took on the task of teaching him that he had to learn all over again how to dress himself. At first it would take him one and a half hours, after which he was so exhausted that he needed a sleep. Even when he first came home, much later, he found dressing very tiring. It was agony watching all these slow processes. My instinct was to rush in and help, but of course that had to be resisted. The only way Leslie was going to get better was by doing things for himself.

To watch the rapport build up between Leslie and the therapists was lovely. They were so encouraging and enthusiastic, as were all the nursing staff. There are so many indignities involved in recovering from a head injury: laughter, as ever, helped. The family and I had organised a rota so that at least one of us would be with Leslie during most of his waking hours, and a list was put up in the office so that the staff would know who to expect. We had been advised that it was still too early for other visitors. So many people wanted to come, but it would have been impossible to admit one without the floodgates opening, a situation which Leslie couldn't have coped with.

Patrick was still dealing with all the press enquiries, and finding it difficult to get through to the media the idea that I really didn't feel like giving any interviews since the future was still too uncertain. His file of letters from the press was getting thicker and thicker: *no* was a word the press didn't seem to understand. A substantial sum, to be paid to any charity that I cared to name, was offered by one editor; but this seemed like blackmail to me, and I declined.

The last thing I needed on getting back from the hospital around nine at night, with washing and mail to cope with, was to find a reporter parked on the drive. But there they were, and on several occasions I also came across them outside the village shop, ready to jump out as I went down in the morning to collect the post I'd redirected there. They were still hanging around at the hospital, too, and I was cross when one came into the canteen while Liz and I were having lunch one day, sat down at our table and later on introduced herself!

On a lighter note, one exciting letter arrived on 18 November, marked 'Urgent and Personal'. It was from the personal secretary to the Prime Minister, and informed us in the strictest confidence that Leslie's name was being submitted to Her Majesty the Queen with a recommendation that she appoint him a Commander of the Most Noble Order of the British Empire. There was a form enclosed to be signed if Leslie was agreeable. He duly appended his signature – the first time he had done so since before his accident. Although he couldn't yet speak, I knew he was thrilled.

The tube in his throat came out at last on Monday, 23 November. Charlotte was there that morning and heard him speak for the first time. His voice was very quiet and rather croaky, which made it difficult to hear him. A week later the nose tube came out, which meant that he could eat soft foods for the first time since the accident. At first the problem with eating was the same as with writing – it was difficult to slow him down. He would fill his mouth to capacity and look like a hamster, then find it difficult to swallow.

On 1 December I got Richard, our hairdresser, to come along to the hospital to cut Leslie's hair. The new growth was getting longer, and it was time to try to marry up the two sides. Leslie was very quiet throughout, and later on he asked for a mirror. It was the first time he had asked to look at himself since the accident, and it occurred to me that maybe he thought his face had been scarred. I had told him several times that he had had a car crash, but it was impossible to tell whether he had really taken it in. The doctors were pretty sure he was still in the state of post-trauma amnesia which follows a period of coma and lasts until the patient regains day-to-day memory.

When I handed Leslie a mirror, he studied himself for quite a while and seemed quite satisfied. Later that day David Sandeman popped in and I told him that Leslie had taken a look at himself.

'What did you think?' David asked him.

There was a long pause before the reply came: 'I've decided not to sue!'

From this time on his progress was rapid, with one exception – his voice, which didn't seem to be getting any louder. It turned out that his throat was tremendously swollen, so we knew there would be no improvement until the swelling subsided.

The time had now arrived to start Leslie back on Warfarin for his heart condition. Getting the right balance of the medication was tricky, and at first he got so breathless that for a few days he stopped going to the stroke unit gym where he was normally treated. Instead the physios visited him in his room and got him standing, supporting him on either side. Dr Pounceford, who was advising on his heart condition, congratulated him on his improvement.

'You're amazing – what do you put it down to?' he asked.

'Grim determination,' was Leslie's reply.

By the second week in December Chris and Sian were trying to get Leslie walking, holding on to the parallel bars in the gym. One of them would walk behind him carrying a chair in case he needed a rest on the way. Not Leslie! He surprised us all by reaching the end before sitting down, and then repeated the exercise three times, whereupon we all applauded.

A few days later Leslie made his first car trip – I drove him just around Frenchay – and then a family meeting was called. His medical condition had improved to such an extent that it was now time to discuss his rehabilitation. After much discussion, and having taken advice from Brian Cummins, the senior neuro-surgeon, it was decided that it would be best for Leslie to stay in his room at Frenchay, continuing with the therapy, until we could get him home. If his present progress were maintained, this might be in another six to eight weeks. It was suggested that nearer the time the physios should visit us at home to see whether any alterations or aids might be needed, after which we would start by getting Leslie home for one night, then for a weekend. This would give me some idea of how I was going to be able to cope.

It must have been very frustrating for Leslie, sitting there and hearing us all discussing him. Brian apologised for not bringing him in more and asked him how he felt. His answer took the form of a very succinct rude word! Later that day he became very argumentative over his supper.

'That's not what I ordered,' he said when I took it in. 'It is, darling,' I replied, pointing to the menu with his name at the top.

'Go and find Mr Leslie,' he said, 'and get me a solicitor.'

Realising that he had meant to say 'sister' rather than 'solicitor', I was laughing with one of the nurses as I went to get him a salad. When I returned he was quite upset and I was really angry with myself, conscious that he must have felt ridiculed, and I apologised. For one who had previously been so articulate it must have been hell.

Christmas was fast approaching and the mail was pouring in. I took down the Get Well cards and replaced them with Christmas cards. They covered every wall of Leslie's room at Frenchay as well as the drawing and dining rooms at home. I realised that immediately after Christmas would come the publication of the New Year's Honours List, and the press would be desperate for some pictures of Leslie. So I asked Dan McAlister, my youngest sister Sarah's son, to come down the week before Christmas with his camera. He arrived at the hospital before lunch on the Saturday morning and his first shots were done in Leslie's room with a wall of cards for background. It was quite amazing to see Leslie's reaction when the camera appeared. When he opened the fridge door and the light came on he always used to say, 'I'll do twenty minutes.' That day it was immediately apparent that the performing instinct was just as ingrained as ever.

On Sunday the 20th we took Leslie home for the first time since the accident. I had put up a Christmas tree in the hall and decorated it, and everything was looking beautiful. Getting him into the house presented no problems – as we had with my wheelchair-bound mother, we avoided the steps and took him in through the garage and back courtyard. For safety's sake, I had booked a nurse to accompany me and to help get Leslie in and out of the car.

For me, that afternoon was one of extremely mixed emotions. The sight of Leslie back in his home surroundings emphasised the gravity of his situation: but I also felt triumphant that we had got him there – something which I would have found inconceivable only a few weeks before. We were home for just over an hour, and then returned to Frenchay.

The following day Brian and Elspet Rix came to the hospital to visit Leslie. He was thrilled, and invited them to the gym where he proudly demonstrated his prowess on the parallel bars. But that evening he was exhausted, and seemed unwell – I think the effects of the past two days' excitement had been building up. I left the hospital at 9 p.m., and at 10.30 the phone rang at home: it was the night staff nurse. She told me that they had taken Leslie for a scan as he had had a fit; she would ring me again later, she said. When she did so, the message was that all was well and he was now sleeping soundly. I had dressed ready to go back to Frenchay, but she said there was no need. All the same, the old butterflies in the tummy were fluttering again and I couldn't sleep. But despite this hitch David Sandeman still thought we would be able to get Leslie home on Christmas Day – and so we did.

It was an odd Christmas. For thirty years Leslie and I had always been the hub round which the family celebrations revolved – usually with fourteen to sixteen sitting down for Christmas dinner. Now there were only five of us awaiting Leslie's arrival – Liz and I, my sister Lesley, Eddie, a widow who had always been my mother's good neighbour, and a past neighbour of ours, Chris Moss.

The ambulance arrived at 12.45, and Ray, the nurse, joined us for lunch. Leslie was still heavily sedated but enjoyed opening his presents. Despite feeling unwell after the fit he had insisted that Liz go out on Christmas Eve and buy me a gold seal for my braclet. I was amazed how he remembered it. Patients who have suffered brain injury and been in a coma spend many weeks after coming round in what is called post-trauma amnesia – they don't really know where they are or what day of the week it is unless you constantly remind them. Leslie still has no memory of that first Christmas after his accident. Anyway the seal was beautiful. The message he had written on the tag was lengthy, though, apart from 'To my Darling Jean', incomprehensible – but I still treasure it. After lunch the rest of the family popped over, but by 3 p.m. it was obvious that Leslie was ready to return to Frenchay.

I didn't go in on Boxing Day – other members of the family took it in turns to be with him while I recharged my batteries. It was the first day I had missed going to Frenchay since 3 October, and I was frankly exhausted. Just before New Year I rang the family to tell them of Leslie's honour, and of course they were all proud and thrilled. I spent New Year's Eve at home with my two younger sisters – we drank to the coming year and I wondered just what it would bring for Leslie and me.

As January arrived I realised that the time had come for me to start to learn a little basic nursing. If Leslie was to come home I had to be able to get him in and out of the car and in and out of bed on my own. So on my return to Frenchay I asked the nurses for a quick Florence Nightingale course! After physio two days later I wheeled him back to his room. Once you got him out of his chair he could support himself as he was now using his Zimmer. We managed this, and then I got him into bed – actually it was more like beaching him! He lay back like a stranded whale, and – bless his heart – he laughed and laughed. I was truly grateful for the laughter – if he had got cross at my ineptitude I should have burst into tears.

On 9 January Liz came down for the weekend. It was a lovely day, so in the afternoon we decided to take Les home on our own. We managed well (the most difficult part was fitting the wheelchair and Zimmer into the car together!) and took him into the house feeling triumphant. It was his first visit home with just us – he sat there and stared all round him.

'Has it changed, Les?' I asked.

There was a pause. 'Not one whit,' came the reply.

Before we left he asked us to get his chair over to the piano, and he played a bit of Chopin's Fantasie Impromptu with his left hand. It was a bit wobbly, but then so was I – the tears were running down my face.

Home Again

The spring of 1993 was early: by the last week of February the daffodils and forsythia were in bloom and there was a smell of newly mown grass in the air at Frenchay. Leslie was now at home, but three times a week I drove him to the hospital for physio, occupational (OT) and speech therapy. Originally the idea had been to make arrangements for these nearer home, but before Leslie was discharged he happened to say to Nicki during an OT session: 'I seem to have drawn the short straw.' Speech still didn't come easily and he would often come out with a sentence at random, making it difficult to work out its relevance.

'In what way, Les?' Nicki asked him.

'Well, I've built up a rapport with all of you.'

I was sitting nearby and the penny dropped. 'Are you saying you don't want to go anywhere else for therapy?'

'Yes,' he replied, and I realised what he meant – coming home was a big step for him, and it would be daunting if on top of this he had to get used to different therapists in new surroundings. We discussed it there and then, and after Nicki had spoken to Brian Cummins a programme was worked out for us: we would come to Frenchay on Tuesdays, Wednesdays and Fridays.

We both found the first month at home exhausting and at times very scary. Leslie was still unsteady on his feet and prone to fall, and I had been warned that another bang on the head at this time could be very serious. The first fall came on the day after he got home. I was helping him back to bed, and when he sat down he was too near the edge. Slowly and gently he slid to the floor, sitting with his back against the side of the bed.

Try as I could, there was no way I was going to be able to get him up on my own. A neighbour, Deidre Horstmann, who is a physio, had left a message on the answerphone: 'Lovely to hear Leslie's home. Let me know if I can be of help any time.' I rang her.

'Hello Jean,' she answered. 'How's Leslie?'

'He's well,' I said, 'but sitting on the floor.'

'I'll be with you in a moment,' was the prompt reply.

Bless her – together we managed to get him to turn on to his knees and then raised him. In his first session at Frenchay, Jill, who had taken over from Sian and Chris now that he was an outpatient, started teaching him how to get up off the floor by himself!

I learned quickly that Leslie couldn't cope with being rushed in any way, so we had to rise early to get him breakfasted and ready to leave for therapy at 9.15. Luckily his Zimmer frame fitted in the bowl of our shower, so that solved bathing problems. We had to allow enough time to wheel him out to the car, load the wheelchair and Zimmer, and unload at the other end. What I desperately needed was some time off, and here I was lucky to have the help of a wonderful nurse called Berenice. She was marvellous with him and a great talker, and together they would put the world to rights.

I abandoned any attempt to be Superwoman, Marks & Spencer became our chef. Having stocked up with their readymade meals, we ate handsomely. I reckon I could now appear on *Mastermind*, making M & S foods my specialised subject!

By the second week in March we were well into a routine, and Leslie was making great advances, spurred on by a goal he had set himself. In January a letter had come from St James's Palace summoning him to an investiture at Buckingham Palace in February, but kindly offering alternative dates, the latest being 21 July. Being quite determined that he would not go to the Palace in a wheelchair, he opted for the July date. Jill knew about this and was helping to get him ready for the great day.

Nicki was still working hard on his right hand and arm and that too was progressing well. In speech therapy Rachel and Jackie got him to keep a journal – something he didn't really enjoy much – but looking back on it now it's quite marvellous to see the improvement he made over the weeks. At the start of February the sentences were short and stark: 'I slept a lot. I wrote thankyou cards. I filled in answers to my homework.' Yes – they gave him homework too! But by April there is a lovely entry: 'Today is the sort of day that makes me feel good to be alive. It is wonderfully sunny, the air is crisp, and the sound of the notes played by the soloist coming up from the radio downstairs on Classic FM all remind me of what I so nearly lost in one minute on the M5.'

On the second Thursday in April I took Leslie down to Communion in our local church – it's a short mid-week service attended by a dozen or so villagers. The gates were opened wide so that I could drive the car in. I wheeled Leslie up the aisle and he stayed in his chair throughout the service; Richard brought the Communion to us.

Friends were coming to visit us, too – Ronnie Barker and Joy, June Whitfield and Tim, Sylvia Syms, Derek and Gillian Iley (Derek had been a boyhood friend of Leslie's and best man at our wedding), and Ann and Norman Burrough (I'd been bridesmaid at their wedding and Ann had been in the Ovaltineys with us). Some of the Taverners who were working in the area came to see us too – Henry Kelly and Nick Parsons – together with Peter and Erica Hughes with Simon, their son, who now plays cricket for Durham and writes about it in the *Independent*.

All of them marvelled at how well Leslie looked, and they were gentle and patient with him when he took time to find words. He used a lot of mime when he couldn't recall the right ones, and I told him it was like living in the midst of *Give Us a Clue* and *Call My Bluff*. All the wit and humour were still there – it was just a bit slower arriving now. Also, he found too many people and long conversations difficult and still became exhausted quickly.

On the first weekend in June I took Les on his first trip to London since the accident, to our flat near Lord's cricket ground. The weather was glorious and I drove with the car windows open, only to see his silk cravat which I had hung up with his shirts fly bird-like through the window and away.

The visit was a great success. It was lucky that Leslie was now able to walk with a stick, as our flat is tiny and a wheelchair would have posed problems. On the Sunday evening we took a walk along St John's Wood Road, rehearsing our walk to Lord's, where we had been invited to join John Paul Getty Junior in his private box later that month. Suddenly a taxi drew up alongside and the cabbie jumped out. 'I thought it was you,' he said. 'Cor, am I glad to see you – you look great!' It was moving and lovely. It happened when I took Leslie out in Keynsham, but somehow I hadn't expected it in London.

The Lord's Test Match started on Thursday, 17 June. Pauline and Brian Johnston – Johnners of *Test Match Special* fame – held a party every year on the Friday of the Lord's Test, and over the past few years we had been lucky enough to be invited. Indeed, the previous year's had also been Johnners' eightieth birthday party. Pauline had sent us an invitation for the 1993 party with a note on the back: 'I know you probably won't be able to make it, but this is to let you know you've not been forgotten.' We knew that already, as dear Brian had been sending a succession of his wonderfully rude Bamforth postcards to Leslie in Ward 2. Unbeknown to me, Leslie had written accepting the invitation, and Pauline rang to say how thrilled she was. We went along for just an hour: what a welcome! It was overwhelming. The *Test Match Special* team and all the cricket luminaries came over to say hello. Leslie was thrilled: it was really our first big outing since the accident, and what could have been better? Two days later we were at Lord's in John Paul Getty Junior's private box. Leslie was in Valhalla.

With the investiture approaching I began to feel slight apprehension about our visit to the Palace. I learned that as soon as you arrived at the entrance there was a grand flight of thirty or more stairs, after negotiating which one would hear the ushers call out: 'Recipients to the right, guests and families straight on.' This would mean that, having negotiated all those stairs, Leslie would have to be abandoned by us. I sat down and wrote to Squadron Leader Sowerby, the gentleman who had written to us earlier, explaining my fears. I told him that, although Les was walking reasonably well, I had dubbed him

'Les the Lurch' (one of the current Australian cricket team was called 'Merve the Swerve') and asked if someone could be delegated to keep an eye on him.

The telephone rang the next morning. It was a lady from the office of the Central Chancery at St James's Palace. 'We are so glad you wrote to us, Mrs Crowther,' she said. 'Another sticker for your car is in the post and this will direct you to the Duke of York's entrance. There is a lift there that Mr Crowther can use, and we have made arrangements for a page to be with him all the time.'

That was such a relief – now we had all the excitement of getting the clothes for the occasion and conducting rehearsals for Leslie, making him walk forwards and backwards. Jill had started him off and I continued at home. I became the Queen and made Leslie walk into the room, stop, bow, walk forward and bend his head so that I could place the ribbon bearing the medal over his head to hang in place – CBEs are worn like this, not pinned on. Then he had to walk backwards, stop, bow and exit to the right. On one occasion he almost fell over because as he bent his head I said (still being the Queen), 'Your flies are undone!' I hoped he wouldn't remember that remark on the day.

We awoke early on 21 July, and at 9.40 the car arrived to take us. The ceremony was wonderful. It had all the colour, pomp and dignity for which the British are so famed, and I felt immensely proud. I can't honestly say I saw the Queen placing the insignia over Leslie's head as too many tears were pouring down my face. I'm glad we bought the video of it all so that we can share it with the rest of the family.

Afterwards Tony, the page, took us up to Prince Edward's apartments to say hello. The Prince had given us the immense pleasure of a visit to Frenchay earlier in the year when he succeeded Leslie as President of the Lord's Taverners. Not only was it a pleasure to see the Prince again, but we also had quite a tour of the Palace.

A quick facing of the cameras, then it was into the car and off to the London Hilton where the rest of the family were waiting. We had the most glorious celebratory lunch in the Window on the World restaurant looking out on to the Palace and grounds we had just left. What a day of joy – one that had seemed an impossibility only a few months before, and one we had been able to share with our beautiful, loving family.

Leslie's promised sixtieth birthday present from me was a trip to Gleneagles, which became a reality in August 1993. As we drove over the Forth bridge the clouds parted and the sun shone, which it continued to do for the next ten days. It was a glorious holiday for both of us.

Walking in the lovely grounds one day, I thanked Les for being there with me and told him how much I admired him for not being bitter and angry at what had happened. There was a pause; then he said, 'I'm just so grateful.' He followed that, of course, with a ribald, unprintable remark and we both laughed.

Returning home at the beginning of September I looked back on the year that had passed. So much had happened, so many things we'd learned. I had felt deep grief and amazing joy; seen immense courage and felt enormous love. When you think you will have no more time together, every day that follows becomes a bonus and a joy.

To my family, friends, fans, Frenchay Hospital,
Clouds House and 10 per cent to Billy Marsh

Part Two

Leslie's Story

Bread-and-Lard Island
1933–44

Nottingham. Noted for Player's cigarettes, Boots the chemists, Raleigh bikes, lace – and pretty girls. The two last are connected: lacemaking provided lots of jobs for women, and fresh-faced country wenches homed in on them.

Once there they found difficulty with the local dialect. For instance, 'Eh up, me duck, keep on causy' is an impassioned plea by a Nottingham adult to a younger member of the family to keep off the road, whilst if a citizen wishes to confuse a casual visitor he or she will say whatever needs saying in a one-word sentence, thus: 'Esezeantgorranyburraberryas' – which, roughly translated, means 'He says he is not in possession of the thing referred to but I am willing to wager that he has it.'

The city is also famous for clarifying the fact that Saturday night is invariably followed by Sunday morning, a phenomenon that was not proven until Alan Sillitoe and Albert Finney put it beyond doubt.

Through the city runs the Trent: broad, sluggish – and warm after flowing past the cooling towers of the several generating stations up-river in what is known as Killowat Valley. *Trent* is reputedly an old Viking word meaning 'marauder', a reminder that the Brian Cloughs of those days rowed up the rivers to do their fell work ('When I find you I'll Trent you', 'I'm under the bridge.')

On the right bank lies the hallowed sward of Trent Bridge cricket ground and west of that, appropriately enough, West Bridgford. Formerly a village in its own right, it has long been

47

a suburb of the city. Yet it still retains vestiges of its former
rusticity and is a pleasant place to live. Suburb and city: each
by turn provided the backdrop against which my early life was
played. West Bridgford was known as Bread-and-Lard Island
by the rest of Nottingham, mainly because by the time you'd
kept up with the Joneses – which in West Bridgford was a
major requirement – you'd be left pretty skint. What you'd
have left after buying your loaf wouldn't buy butter but good,
old-fashioned lard, which you'd spread on thickly. And you
could top that off with tripe and onions. A scurrilous story used
to be told of a conversation between two West Bridgfordians:

He: 'Oh! I see you've hung up the new curtains.'
She: 'Yes, well I thought I might.'
He: 'Pity.'
She: 'Why?'
He: 'I hadn't finished reading 'em yet.'

Number 7 Victoria Road, West Bridgford is where my parents,
Leslie Senior and Ethel, were living when I was born on 6
February 1933 – the same shameful year, as Barry Cryer was
later to point out, in which Hitler came to power. (I've forgiven
him now – Barry, that is, not Hitler.)

Eighteen months later all that sham was left behind when
my parents spotted a sub-post office-cum-corner shop in the
city and saw it as the answer to an ambitious married couple's
prayer – and more particularly as the possible source of the
wherewithal to fit out young Leslie, when the time should
come, in the togs of Nottingham High School, and furnish
the necessary fees. The shop was a conf/tob – a confectioner's
and tobacconist's – and there was just one snag: it was in the
Meadows, an area of Nottingham which did not, at least in
those days, live up to its name. Number 147 Wilford Crescent
East not only fronted on to the road: it opened on to it. The
front garden was the street, in which I played happily.

When the time for school arrived I would catch the plum- and
orange-coloured bus which made its way along Arkwright
Street to Old Market Square. From there I walked up Theatre
Street, along the Arboretum, and so to the High School. At
that seat of learning I earned the nickname 'dormouse' because

I was asleep most of the time. I was probably exhausted by my various escapades on the way to school including, in season, ploughing through the chestnut leaves which the Arboretum gardeners would have swept into neat and tidy piles, and running away from them armed with a great mass of conkers.

Nottingham High School was – and still is, I believe – the city's top school for boys; in my day mostly peopled by the progeny of the posh. In their contacts with the school and the homes of the boys to whose parties I was invited (inevitably swankier than ours in The Meadows) my parents, brought up in the world of showbusiness, must have seen a great contrast. Which reminds me that I have yet to introduce them as they stand patiently there in the wings.

My father Leslie was a big man with a voice to match, trademark of his profession as an actor which had carried him uncertainly through the period of his early manhood – since, in fact, the First World War, traces of which were still emerging from his skin in the form of shrapnel when he shaved. He never talked about his experiences in the war, or indeed much about his past life at all. Years later I came to understand why!

My mother Ethel, who in my book had more right to the wing-space, was a complete contrast. Small and shy, though with a will of steel when demanded, she had been a stage manager with the Compton Comedy Company until her marriage. This, one of the numerous small touring companies of those days, had been founded by the father of Fay and Nell; Mother was proud of her connection with Fay Compton, who achieved considerable fame as a stage, film and radio actress.

Ethel was the eldest of three sisters, the next being Norah and the youngest Helen, nicknamed Bunty. Mother's second Christian name, an exotic one for those days, was Maraquita. I often wondered how Granny could have come by such a name, as she was even tinier and quieter than her eldest daughter. I see her now, grey hair wrapped round her face to be caught in a bun at the back, tiny body cocooned in a grey shawl which was secured by a clasp. Maraquita, indeed!

My paternal Granny was just the opposite – (the epitome of the Victorian grandmama – she would sit, stiff as a ramrod in her chair, grey hair pulled together at the top in a bun and fastened with a comb. As a small boy I was particularly fascinated by her skinny neck which emerged tortoise-like from a high lace collar. Her husband Frederick George, my paternal grandfather, had at one time been secretary to a mining company.

Uncle Ernest, my father's brother, lived with his mother in Lewisham in south London and was aptly named since he'd got religion really badly. I'll never forget a trip to Greenwich Naval Museum, the object of which was to conduct young Leslie round the exhibits and generally improve his knowledge of matters maritime. Alas, no sooner had an unsuspecting couple hove into sight than Ernest sprang into action, pulled a bundle of tracts out of his pocket and began to sound off about what Jesus could do for their lives would they but take Him to their bosoms. All this while I, hot with embarrassment, crouched behind a display cabinet. Eventually he returned to me, as hot as I was but in his case with zealous fervour, and I had hopes that our perambulation might resume. But it was not to be: no sooner had he spotted another couple than he was off again. No sort of treat for a young boy!

They really were an extraordinary family. Dad's sister Enid collected weapons of war, and festooned round the walls were assegais, Masai shields, knobkerries – the lot. The sanest person among them was the man she'd married – Uncle Harold, a bank manager but otherwise decent. He was also an honorary steward at the Albert Hall and as such the recipient of complimentary tickets, which on occasions he would generously present to Mother who was into all things artistic and passed on her love of music, painting and books to me. In this way we were privileged to hear Tito Gobbi and to enjoy other musical treats.

Mum and Dad had met at Leigh-on-Sea in Essex at the town's repertory company and married on 25 January 1932 at Rochford. It was Dad's second marriage, but he kept so quiet about his first that I knew nothing about it until 1963 when, well into the run of *The Black and White Minstrel Show* at the Victoria Palace, someone named Ron called at the stage door and asked to see me. As he walked into my dressing room I had a tremendous shock – it was as if Dad had suddenly come in. He turned out to be my father's only child from his first marriage, and was about ten years my senior. Unfortunately we had only thirty minutes before the second show began so we arranged to meet later on when Ron, his wife Win and their son Tony called round to tea with the family. We've only met once more when Ron and his family came to see me in my last pantomime at Croydon in 1989, but we always exchange news at Christmas. I hope we'll renew the acquaintance now that I'm not dashing around so much.

Soon after my parents were married my father retired, arguing that the advent of the talkies would kill the theatre – about as daft a prediction as that of the Hollywood producer who turned down *Gone with the Wind* on the ground that the public wouldn't be able to stand another war picture! This was a turning point in their relationship and they began to argue, my father directing the rich boom of his voice at my mother, who would shriek back at him. Sometimes she would come into my bedroom, break down and sob uncontrollably in my arms as I tried to comfort her. Often I would bury my head under the pillows in an attempt to shut out this insane warfare.

At the age of four or five I used to get a recurrent nightmare in which my father would be standing at the far end of an otherwise empty room shouting across a wide gap in the floor – an abyss of blackness. These would have a devastating effect on me and I would wake up screaming.

There were lulls in the hostilities. I remember one occasion when Dad fell off a high stool in our small kitchen while fiddling with the net curtain. He broke his leg and had to go to hospital. Mum couldn't do enough for him while he was there – she still loved him, you see. But no sooner was he home than they started their screaming matches again, and my nightmares returned.

In discussing our respective fathers my neighbour Graham and I have discovered that they had a 'little problem' in common. He delicately put it that, far from his dad being a teetotaller, he totally abhorred tea. I put it more bluntly, since I inherited my father's problem. He was, and I am, an alcoholic.

THE DEADLY DISEASE

Alcoholism. A little-known terminal disease which leaves its victim dead – not, as you might imagine, lying in a gutter clad in a grubby raincoat and clutching an empty bottle, but dead to the world or as near as dammit, remembering – or failing to remember – the cycle of events which led to this pass. Such as what it was like before you took that fateful first drink, regretting it but at the same time, and uppermost in your mind, knowing that you must have another drink. The awful cycle of events that if not checked eventually leads to the abyss.

ALCOHOLICS ANONYMOUS

The only club in the world which holds the cure – and even they say that there is no real cure. Just don't pick up that first drink. Simple as that. If you don't drink you can't get drunk. Just rely on the encouragement of other club members and respond in kind.

End of lesson.

Back to Pop, whom we find steadily drinking away the savings which both had struggled so earnestly to accumulate, even failing to bring home the money he earned as a sorting clerk at the GPO, a job he'd taken on after his abrupt retirement from the stage and which he was to stick with for the rest of his life. Mother, of course, ran the shop and was in every other way the driving force of the family. It's an awful business. Until I got to grips with my problem with the help of Alcoholics Anonymous I could see the same sort of thing happening to Jean, who took on the same hunted role as my mother.

Anyway, Leslie senior and Ethel would slag on regardless of what was happening in the outside world, calling a truce only during the summer holidays at Mablethorpe on the Lincolnshire coast, where for three weeks, over a period of five years up to the outbreak of the Second World War, we lived the life of Riley. Based in our rented beach hut, we would play for hours on the sands where my father would transform himself from seasoned drinker to perfect dad, sculpting colossal cars from the sand and leading myself and my delighted beach pals on expeditions among the dunes, 'hunting for Jack'. In this game the beaches became the great Australian Outback, and such was my father's vivid imagination that he could persuade us impressionable boys that the hunt for 'Jack' was for real, and that any stray dogs who were tagging along out of curiosity were dingoes, to be avoided at all costs. What other holidaymakers thought as we rent the air with shouts of 'Coo-ee' in our quest for the elusive Jack I daren't think.

Back in The Meadows, the aggravation at home and tedium at school were alleviated by my developing love affair with the piano. Like many other families – though by no means all – we had an 'upright' in the front room, something which earned Mother and Father my eternal gratitude. It's no exaggeration to say that I took to it from the start – and it took to me. But it was Veronica Brown who transformed my infant tinklings into the magic of music.

Miss Brown lived just up the road from us, on the opposite side, and regularly from the age of five young Leslie would trot dutifully along to do, under her benevolent supervision, Czerny exercises, which were designed to make the fingers more agile and the piano more boring. Then back home I would hare to perform more flamboyant works, a simplified version of the solo part of Tchaikovsky's first piano concerto being a favourite.

From small acorns do great oak trees grow (I wasn't born near Sherwood Forest for nothing!). It was as a direct consequence of my musical development that we eventually moved to London, where it would be possible for me to take up a junior scholarship for the pianoforte at the Royal Academy of Music. Had this not happened, my whole life would have taken a different course.

Music apart, the routine of life in The Meadows was alleviated from time to time by visits to my Auntie Bunty, who lived at Spring Hill, a palatial Queen Anne residence in Walsall, Staffordshire. Auntie Bunty had married well: hence the huge house set in its own grounds, the complete antithesis to 147 Wilford Crescent East.

There was a story attached to Spring Hill – perhaps apocryphal, though I readily believed it. During the Battle of Britain a German pilot was supposed to have baled out after his aircraft had been hit and had come to earth on the Spring Hill tennis courts, there to be arrested by a quavery Uncle Frazer-Wood, Auntie Bunty's husband, armed with a First World War revolver. Confronted by this gun-toting spectacle, the poor chap must have thought his last hour had come. But he needn't have worried. My uncle invited him into the dining room, brought out the brandy bottle, and they both got pissed, after which the old boy said: 'Well, you know what I'm going to do now, don't you?'

'Turn me over to the authorities?' the other tentatively suggested.

'Right,' replied his host, and duly did so.

Being an only child, I had to rely heavily on my cousins for close companionship, and I had two particular favourites. Mary Rose, Auntie Bunty's daughter, was a ravishing girl and we spent many happy hours playing cowboys and Indians in the grounds of Spring Hill. Then there was Wally, a day younger than me. He lived with his parents in the village of Sawley, on the Trent near Nottingham. Sawley was to come in for unmerited punishment during the war when British boffins bent the Luftwaffe's directional radio beam away from the Rolls-Royce works at Derby, putting Sawley on the spot as recipient of tons of bombs, which did the war effort no harm but sorely afflicted the villagers.

Sadly, Wally's parents were both deaf mutes. He, happily, was unafflicted and was a great companion. We shared many interests – silent films, stamp collecting, swimming and Mary Rose, though even at that age we were aware of the perils of consanguineous relations and so we concentrated on the swimming!

There was plenty of that in both the Trent and the Thames. Auntie Bunty had pulled off a master-stroke by flirting with a big businessman to such effect that he lent her his sea-going cruiser *Nephatite*, moored on the Thames just below Oxford. Here Wally and I spent many a blissful hour learning to overcome our fear of depths by paddling across the width of the river, supported not only by car inner tubes but also by youth's inner sense of security.

I don't know when Wally started to swim but I know when I did. It was at Carrington Lido in Nottingham where I swam from the deep-end steps to the nearest point on the side rails – a difficult manoeuvre as it entailed going out to sea, as it were, and doubling back to 'shore'. I've been in the deep end many times since then, but I'll never forget the thrill of that first solo swim. It was as though I'd conquered the world.

The third of my cousins was Stanley, son of mother's brother Fred. He later got engaged to the only daughter of the headmaster of Nottingham High School, so I suppose he was the real success of the family. But he nursed a passion stronger even than for his intended. Stanley possessed a model theatre which he not only wired for lighting but provided with scenes. Years later he became an editor for the film director David Lean, and I'd like to think it was he who did the cutting on that magical scene where Magwitch the convict springs up before the young Pip, a confrontation which shocked whole audiences out of their seats.

With these welcome diversions our life in The Meadows rolled onwards like the broad and placid Trent, oblivious as we were, like many in Britain, to the real strength of the storm gathering over Europe. But not for long. Hitler's invasion of Poland in the summer of 1939 effectively put an end to the dithering thirties. Not only that, but soon after he marched into Poland we marched back to West Bridgford, leaving The Meadows for ever. It came about in the following way.

The actual declaration of war found us in Mablethorpe, where the early September sunshine couldn't disperse the chill of apprehension in the air which, young as I was, I could sense. We were listening to the wireless in the beach hut when Neville Chamberlain's voice came over: '. . . No such assurance having been received, we are now at war with Germany. . . .' Like thousands of other mothers in the land, mine was crying, and Father, though stiff-upper-lipped, doubtless harboured grave thoughts. As for me, at seven years old I was terrified – I always am when I don't know what's round the corner.

Almost immediately the summer beaches began taking on the sterner guise of war, with soldiers laying land mines, erecting barbed wire entanglements and putting out of bounds my happy summer playground. Then back we holidaymakers went, pursued by a phantom invasion army which in the event never did disturb the deserted wartime beaches, back on Midland Red coaches to Nottingham and, in our case, to Wilford Crescent East. Soon after our return, Lord Haw-Haw's grating tones over the wireless opened a new chapter for us. 'Germany calling. . . . Germany calling. . . . We know about that munitions factory in The Meadows, Nottingham. . . .'

That was enough. Even lard was preferable to bombs. We packed up and returned to West Bridgford – but not to the same house. We sat out the first years of the war in the comparative safety of 12 George Road, at which address I followed the ebb and flow of the various battle lines and lost count of the number of times Mersa Matruh changed hands.

I say 'comparative safety' because Nottingham happened to be surrounded by airfields, mostly occupied by fighter squadrons: Plumtree, Tollerton, East Bridgford, Syerston – and lots more. So there was plenty for the Luftwaffe to go at, and go at it they did during that phase of the Battle of Britain when Goering was trying to put the RAF out of action. On one particular night he threw his bombers against all the airfields simultaneously in a grand-slam operation calculated to neutralise the defence. Unfortunately for the bombers they were got at by the occupants of these hornets' nests and the inevitable happened: many of the raiders scattered, jettisoning their loads of high explosives and incendiaries indiscriminately.

It was then that Nottingham had a taste of the fare that was being dished out night after night in London and other prime targets. As wave after wave of bombers droned overhead, engines labouring from the weight of bombloads, young Leslie rapidly revised his assessment of Number 12's safety factor. When the bombs began to fall the screaming noise deliberately built into the design to add to the terror certainly succeeded so far as I was concerned.

The pockets of devastation left by the fleeing bombers were not confined to the city but extended to the suburbs – including

At two years old,
with my mother.

My father, Leslie
Senior, in younger
days.

A rare 'happy snap' of the
Crowthers, Mablethorpe, 1937.

One of the sand cars my father built.

One the selectors forgot!

Nottingham High School Star Pupil, 1939.

Evacuated to Rothesay. With Christina – an early crush.

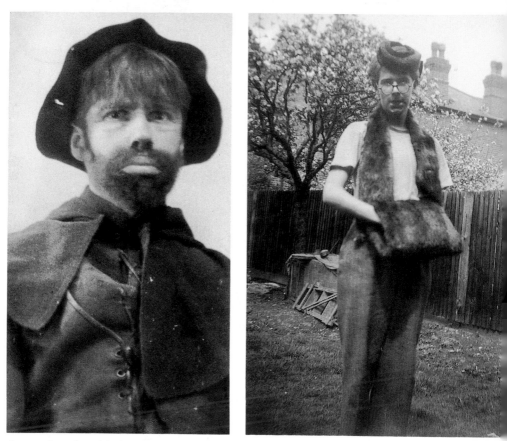

An early role: third watchman in *Much Ado About Nothing*, 1949. The title describes my performance.

No comment, 1949.

In the bushes with the fairies: Regent's Park production of *A Midsummer Night's Dream*, 1951. Jean is on the right.

Home at 225
Richmond Road.

Wedding of the Year,
1953.

An early panto appearance as Idle Jack, Richmond theatre, 1953.

With Kathleen West and Jack Tripp in the Fol-de-Rols.

Appearing in
Crackerjack
in the
afternoon. . .

On stage
with *The
Black and
White
Minstrels* in
the
evening. . .

Learning the scripts in
between.

The Queen's visit to
Crackerjack. From left:
Harry Secombe, Albert
Saveen, Pip Hinton,
Peter Glaze, Gillian
Comber, Eamonn
Andrews.

Christmas with the
family, 1965.

ours – and naturally I was eager to gawk at these in the light of day. The trouble was that the raiders, in their infinite wisdom, had deposited delayed action bombs at all the exits from George Road and these were sufficient to deny me egress to get to school so that, in the words of Hamlet, I was forced to absent myself from felicity awhile.

The following morning at school assembly the headmaster, gazing with pride at his charges, declared that on the morning after the horrific raid one boy, and one boy only, had failed to turn up. As he said this the spotlight of his gaze was beamed upon me. Pointless for me to attempt an explanation. I can still feel the icy wind of contempt which was directed at me.

There was another, and for me no less dramatic, consequence of that night of mayhem. In summer I was accustomed to walk with Mother over the West Bridgford suspension bridge to a sandy patch on the bank of the Trent and there jump in. Performing this trick shortly after the raid, I received a nasty shock. A bomb had scooped out a bloody great hole in the river bed into which I disappeared – this before my solo swimming effort in Carrington Lido.

I vividly recall bobbing up and down and thinking, 'I'm drowning.' Also the odd sensation, when I came up for air, of finding the Trent's choppy surface at eye level. And I can still see my mother dancing up and down on the embankment, and hear her screams. Fortunately these attracted the attention of a passer-by who tore off his jacket, dived in and rescued me. I've often wondered whether he would have done it if he'd known what he was letting the world in for.

With the return to West Bridgford the struggle to make ends meet was resumed – Mother still shouldering the main burden, Dad having squandered on booze what should have been his contribution. She took up a house-to-house insurance round and would leave home at 5 a.m. to go cycling along the village lanes to collect the weekly dues. That people were up at this time seems unbelievable now, but this was wartime when many people were on shiftwork producing armaments, or were engaged in fire watching or Home Guard duties.

Returning at 7 a.m., she would cook breakfast for Dad and

me before his departure for the post office and mine for school – or for a music lesson. It still breaks me up to think of the hardships she endured to give me every chance of success, and whenever I've made a particular balls-up of anything I've imagined her looking down in horror. Through all this Dad was still on the drink, pouring it down his throat just as fast as he earned it – and the rows continued. But there was one magical moment – it would be when I was about eight – which stands out from the domestic gloom.

Whatever the difficulties, we always went to the pantomime at the Theatre Royal round about Christmastime – and had good seats. On this occasion we were sitting in the front row of the dress circle enjoying *Dick Whittington*, starring Nat Mills and Bobbie. Nat had just reached the time-honoured spot when the song-sheet was let down from the flies for the community sing-along. This involved getting a member of the audience up on stage to help lead the singing. Nat was having difficulty: no one would budge. Suddenly Dad's voice boomed out, double forte:

'Now then lass, I'll give you a hand.'

Nat, dressed as the dame, stood stock still, thought for a moment, then invited him down. No sooner the word than the blow. Before you could say 'Dick Whittington', Dad had joined him on stage.

I suppose one pro recognised the other. Anyway, Nat was about to hand the whole bag of tricks over to Father when the latter pulled a master-stroke. Making a show of donning his spectacles, he declared: 'I must have a look at the libretto', at the same turning his back on both Nat and the audience. He then proceeded to declaim, still in his actor's voice:

'You push the damper in, you pull the damper out, and the smoke goes up the chimney just the same.'

By this time the audience was in hysterics and Nat very wisely, knowing he was licked, kept mum and presented Dad to the audience. And did they applaud him? They did! I stole a glance at Mother, who was busy applauding with the rest – though unlike the rest she was also crying.

Youthful illnesses, particularly of the infectious variety, seemed more common in those days than they are now and were apt to be more serious. Scarlet fever, now almost unknown in Britain, was particularly endemic, and when one day the ambulance came to collect me it was scarlet fever which the doctor had diagnosed. It turned out to be tubercular meningitis, which was bad enough, but incarcerated in an isolation ward full of children whose sins were scarlet I quickly succumbed. The doctor soon realised his mistake and set about trying to cure me of the scarlet fever before tackling the underlying problem. During one night, it was said, I turned blue, and the night nurse had to turn me over and smack some life back into me – a thrill which I was in no shape to appreciate.

All this was pretty agonising for my parents as well as for me. Since it was an isolation ward they weren't allowed in, but had to peer through glass at their suffering son and heir. There was one bright spot. On each visit Dad would bring me in a Dinky toy, and I ended up with quite a collection. The brightness wore off when I realised that they too were isolated and I couldn't take the bloody things with me when I was discharged. Years later, when we needed the money, it took my fancy to return to the hospital and collar them. But I never did. Toys being what they are, I doubt very much whether they would have survived.

Fresh Fields

Soon after my recovery, at the age of eleven I won a Royal Academy of Music scholarship as a Junior Exhibitioner. All hail to Veronica Brown! This entitled me to free piano and theory lessons on Saturday mornings at the Academy, and if I was to take this up it would mean moving near to the RAM in London. Mother, who was by now more firmly in the driving seat than ever, decided that I *should* take it up. To this end she made up her mind to call on Auntie Bunty, who had by then moved with Uncle Frazer-Wood into Cholmondeley Lodge, a villa by the Thames at Richmond which was no less attractive than Spring Hill.

It was Mother's intention to buy a not-too-expensive house in the Twickenham area. She reckoned that with the V1s and V2s which were by then arriving over the capital in increasing numbers she would get a snip, since there was more keenness to get out of the London area than in. This proved to be the case. Towards the end of 1944 she found a largish, detached house in Twickenham with a generous garden and put in hand the selling of the Nottingham house and negotiations for a mortgage on the new one, so that come the end of the war all would be ready for us to make the move – which duly came to pass.

But that is to anticipate. First we had to get to Auntie Bunty's There was no money for train fares, and of course road transport for civilians was almost nil. It may seem strange that we were travelling to London with the intention of buying a new home and yet didn't have the ready cash for a rail fare. I often wondered how mother managed, what with my school fees, the mortgage payments and – above all – the constant drain on the family resources due to Dad's boozing. The necessary was almost always in short supply, and yet Mum always seemed capable of pulling something out of the hat when the occasion demanded. Anyway, our only option on this occasion was to cycle. It was a hundred miles or so, quite a ride for an eleven-year-old boy, let alone his forty-nine-year-old mother, but there was no alternative. So, leaving Dad behind to look after the house, we set off down the A60, London Road.

Through the village of Bunny we pedalled and then into Northamptonshire, through sleepy Milton Keynes (its residents blissfully unaware of what was in store for them), Dunstable, and on through Whipsnade where the hill took such a toll that we decided to pack it in at Watford and take the tube which fortunately, then as now, connects to Richmond via Willesden Junction.

We arrived at Auntie Bunty's bushed, but not too exhausted to gaze in awe at the opulently furnished rooms and walls hung with pictures – one of which, positioned below a skylight, was an original Murillo (I mention this only because it features later). At this time Auntie Bunty had a coterie of theatrical talent shacking up with her, tolerated by long-suffering Uncle Frazer-Wood who, still hopelessly in love with her, could deny her nothing and seemed reasonably content so long as he was allowed to play contract bridge, an obsession which he pursued in the library.

Those who are familiar with the Gate Theatre in Dublin will recognise names such as Hilton Edwards, Michael Mac Liammoir, Cyril Cusack and F.J. McCormick. These, and more, were busy availing themselves of Auntie's hospitality. There was also a young Welsh poet living in with his wife, whom he called The Pig, and his children, referred to as The Piglets. A bastard to his wife and little better to his children, he himself went by the name of Dylan Thomas.

Mother and I managed as far as possible to avoid contact with this bizarre band of interlopers, and on a day early in 1944 this chapter of our odyssey (and very nearly the whole book) was likely to be abruptly terminated. We were taking the air along a stretch of the noble Thames near Cholmondeley Lodge when we noticed a V1 'doodlebug' rocket overhead, seemingly pursuing us. Suddenly its motor cut out, and in the awful silence which followed we stared, fascinated, as the thing dived towards us, filling the horizon. Then we flung ourselves to the ground against the red brick wall which runs along the river at that point, and waited for the end. Deflected by a last-minute puff of wind, the doodlebug landed behind the wall and crashed with an earth-shaking explosion on to a US military hospital, killing 150 patients and staff.

The wall quivered, but held – and still stands as it has since Tudor times, guarding Richmond Palace. We picked ourselves up and ran back to Cholmondeley Lodge. There we found that the glass had been blown from the skylight by the blast and had gashed the Murillo from side to side. Not only that, but the library ceiling had caved in, covering Uncle Frazer-Wood with lath and plaster. Apparently he had remained in his chair, his five cards still fanned out in his hand, enquiring of his partners, who had taken refuge under the table: 'Well, aren't we going to finish this bloody game?'

All this was enough for Mother, who was soon on the phone to the authorities asking that she and her son be evacuated to a place of greater safety.

'Why not go back to Nottingham?' they suggested, a proposal which she immediately rejected on the grounds that (a) it was just as dangerous and (b) we were skint and couldn't afford the return fare anyway.

Their response to this was to ask whether she knew of any address in Scotland which might accommodate us. If so, they added, they would gladly stump up the second-class train fare.

She didn't, but, not to be outdone, gathered me up and swept into the nearest general post office where she demanded a telephone directory for the Glasgow area. This having been produced, she pulled out her hat-pin and stuck it into the middle of a random page, transfixing one William Ritchie, a farmer on the Isle of Bute. 'We know him,' this intrepid lady said to the authorities.

The train fare was duly coughed up and we were soon on our way out of harm's way, though I must admit that as our confrontation with the unknown Mr Ritchie drew nearer our hearts were full of dread, a feeling which intensified after we

63

had left the ferry and proceeded to drag our bicycles up the steep cart-track leading to the farm. We eventually hove into the midden, to find the rugged figure of 'Uncle Wullie' astride the porch.

He regarded us suspiciously. 'Well?'

I gulped and plunged in: 'We are your evacuees for the duration of the war.'

Unperturbed, he shifted his bulk: 'Is that so? Och, well, you'd better come in then. Park your bikes.'

Thus unostentatiously began a friendship with the Ritchie family which has continued to this day. Years later, after our twins were born, Jean and I lost little time in introducing them to our friends in Bute. And later still, when I had achieved what the world is pleased to call 'celebrity status', I was invited to be guest speaker at a civil ceremony in Bute honouring the forces based there during the war. My speech seemed to go down well with all concerned, including members or ex-members of the British, US, Danish, Canadian and Norwegian forces.

Mother and I took to life on the farm and I think we did our bit, especially mother, who deployed her culinary prowess to great effect – her apple pies were particularly appreciated. I would bring the cows home from the fields at night by leading the bull by its nose-ring; the ladies, of course, obediently followed.

From our hillside vantage point on the isle we could look down on the Firth of Clyde, where the traffic of war ceaselessly came and went. Down there, as D-Day approached, they were working on a puzzling construction which later turned out to have been Mulberry Harbour – the prefabricated system of jetties and moles which was later towed across to the Normandy beaches as an aid to the landing of men and supplies for the thrust inland.

Strangely, Mulberry had a direct connection with Bath, the city I later fell in love with and near which we now live. Much of the planning for the D-Day landings, including the floating harbour concept, took place in one of Bath's principal schools where blueprints can still be seen proudly hanging in the great hall. Generals Eisenhower, Montgomery and de Gaulle were present at a discussion of the plans for the harbour when the question was asked: 'What do we call it?' At that point General Eisenhower, happening to glance through the window, noticed a magnificent tree. 'What is the name of that tree?' he asked, and was told that it was a mulberry tree. *Eh voilà*!

Then, astonishingly soon, the war in Europe was over. VE Day was celebrated in May 1945, after which we said a sad goodbye to the hospitable Ritchies and travelled south to Twickenham where mother had succeeded in buying her house – 225 Richmond Road – in the sure hope, faithfully justified in the event, that it would survive all that Hitler could throw at it in the way of V1s and V2s. Mind you, he did his best with more conventional weapons. A bomb which had exploded in Marble Hill Park, opposite our house, might well have seen it off. Fortunately all it did was blow the dustbins over, scattering their contents and flattening the wall at the end of the garden, which was duly repaired by the authorities.

Once in Twickenham Mother started rearing turkeys for the table, filling the now secure back garden with poults which she hoped would grow fat during the summer and come to perfection for the Christmas market. But turkey farming wouldn't bring in enough to clear the mortgage on the Nottingham house, sold for £1,200, and raise a larger one for 225 Richmond Road, which cost £1,500. Some other financial source would have to be found if we were to keep the new roof over our heads. The answer was to be PGs – paying guests – with whom Mother commenced to fill the nine rooms of the house that were surplus to our requirements.

In the summer of 1945, the sale of the Nottingham house having been completed, Dad came to live with us again. During the war separation of husband and wife, parents and children had become almost the norm for many people, and travelling restrictions discouraged inessential journeys. In our case, however, it has to be said that Dad's continued drinking had widened the gulf between him and Mother to an almost unbridgeable extent, a situation which the enforced separation had underlined. To put it bluntly, Mother and I felt somewhat liberated on our own, and doubtless Father also experienced some relief from the tension which was ever present when we were together.

Certainly, once we joined forces again we tended to pursue our separate interests. Father resumed employment as a GPO sorting clerk, this time at Richmond, and settled himself into a comfortable relationship with the landlord of a nearby corner pub. As for Mother and me, despite the perennial cash flow problems we managed to hear a lot of music and see a great deal of theatre during our all-too-few years together at 225 Richmond Road.

We joined the gallery queues to watch Vic Oliver in *The Night and the Music* at the London Coliseum and went many, many times, to the New Theatre in St Martin's Lane to see that miraculous Old Vic company, many of whom had returned from the armed forces to put on classical repertory during those never-to-be-forgotten post-war seasons. From our gallery eyrie we were privileged to witness magical performances by the cream of British theatrical talent: Laurence Olivier, Ralph Richardson, Sybil Thorndike, Lewis Casson, Margaret Leighton, Sir Cedric Hardwicke, Harcourt Williams, Charles Leno, Joyce Redman and many others, performing in classics such as *Oedipus Rex* and *The Critics* – two one-acters on the same night. I also remember seeing the first night of *Richard III* in which Laurence Olivier gave the definitive performance.

In 1946 Mother had saved enough from the PG income to take me on holiday to Paris and Switzerland – another example of her financial legerdemain. I stayed in French youth hostels and Swiss *Jugendherbergen* while Mother put up where she could – on one occasion gaily turning up at a hostel and putting over such a sob story about being broke that the wardens took her in and housed her in one of their palatial residences! We travelled the continent like this and Mum even did the exchange fiddle, swapping pound notes for French francs and then into Swiss francs, and with what we gained we got round Paris, including the Louvre, on a shoestring and even came home with some surplus money!

Young Leslie, meanwhile, was continuing his piano studies at the RAM while pursuing studies of a more general kind at Thames Valley Grammar School in Twickenham, a co-educational establishment at which I discovered, among other things, WOMEN and SEX. Like most little boys I had developed a healthy interest in the opposite sex and spent hours wondering what they looked like undressed. Not having sisters had made me a bit backward in this department. Toddlers splashing in the sea or paddling pools didn't count. It was girls in the playground of about one's own age who were the targets for mental stripping.

I'd had my first break at the age of eight when a nubile young lady of the same age – or maybe a year or two older – virtually picked me up during the school holidays and invited herself round to tea. After tea Mother suggested that we go upstairs to play in my bedroom, a proposition which Deidre Bosworth (you see – I remember her name!) accepted eagerly. Once aloft, she offered me a tour of inspection which I breathlessly accepted. Discarding blouse and vest, she indicated the two pink pimples on her chest: 'These are called "breasts".' I was not impressed, having seen fat boys in the showers better endowed than she was.

Some four years later, at Thames Valley School, as I contemplated the infinitely shapelier forms of the girl pupils, the urge to gratify my curiosity became irrestistible and I formed MY PLAN. This centred on the public swimming baths, where both girls and boys went for swimming lessons and where the changing rooms were separated by a wooden screen which stopped short of ground level. I bought a pocket mirror and instructed my mates to do likewise. At the next opportunity we placed the mirrors in a row under the screen and, skilfully tilting them, we saw – the Lot.

The following week we were surprised to hear sounds of uncontrolled mirth from the other side of the screen. Glancing down, we saw a row of alien mirrors tilted towards our weedy little bodies. It wasn't the retaliation which hurt so much as the laughter.

Sad Endings and New Beginnings

Norman Guest, an inspired history teacher at Thames Valley School, also had the inspiration – whether by design or accident I shall never know – to cast me as 'Higgins the Highwayman of Cranford' in an end-of-term school play. I took to the part with wild enthusiasm, but more than that I put heart and soul into ensuring that the *tout ensemble* should be sensationally successful. And so it was. I booked seats for my parents and I can still hear Father's bellow echoing round the school hall as I strutted my brief hour upon the stage.

My performance must have impressed them because shortly afterwards, following consultations with Auntie Bunty, they decided to send me to drama school – of the sort which also dispensed the less dramatic but no less essential all-round education. Astonishingly, my first reaction was against it. I didn't want to go, I'd only been in Twickenham a year and didn't relish another change of school. However I agreed and arrived in September 1946 at the Cone-Ripman School in Lees Place, Mayfair (now the Arts Educational Trust) full of apprehension. But I soon found my feet, being that rare phenomenon – a boy who actually *liked* acting.

It was from here that I was introduced to radio drama: the BBC Schools Repertory Service had a contract with Cone-Ripman to supply young actors, and I was an early recruit. This was an awe-inspiring experience, because I was appearing (if that is the word) with fully fledged dramatic actors such as Charles Leno, Betty Hardy, Gladys Young,

69

Lockwood West (father of Timothy West) and many others who up till then had been mere voices to me.

Most of them weren't above having a bit of a giggle while rehearsing, or even on the air – a dangerous propensity in the days when all radio was live. But who could have kept a straight face while declaiming lines such as 'Hush! The Le Pissing Indians are coming' in a programme about a little-known North American tribe? Preston Lockwood, another BBC rep stalwart, had to narrate an even worse giggle-inducer during an early science fiction saga. The director, who specialised in space-type sound effects, had arranged for an ultra-realistic farting noise to be sounded as a prelude to the immortal line: 'You will know that I am just passing an asteroid.' Experienced professionals could be seen stuffing hankies into their mouths as mirth-mufflers.

Another peculiar aspect of educational broadcasting in those days was that you had to enunciate your words slowly, at what was called 'schools pace'. This was because reception on some of the early wireless sets was dodgy, and I suppose that the average school set would hardly have been state of the art. Unfortunately schools pace could only emphasise the banality of many of the scripts.

But the schools pace at the Cone-Ripman School was decidedly the opposite. I felt wanted, and, as any professional will tell you, that is the single most important thing in an actor's life. I was no sooner enrolled as a pupil than I was involved in the third-year productions, the reason being that when I joined they were a bit short of men; as a result, young as I was, I was offered men's parts and had the pick of them.

And pick them I did, from a dissolute drip in *Call It a Day* to Benjamin Disraeli in John Drinkwater's play of the same name. But the most important part that came my way at the Cone-Ripman was one for which I shall be eternally grateful: the moon-struck admirer of a rather frail but striking girl with a trace of Somerset in her voice, whom I found myself standing next to in the lunch queue one day, piquante in a ballet leotard. This was Jean, and it was to be a part for life, since we were subsequently thrown together so frequently that we decided we'd better get married. And so we did: this year, 1994, is our fortieth wedding anniversary. Who said it wouldn't last?

At Easter 1948 Mummy and I took off for a treat in the form of a trip to Ireland, visiting my cousin Mary Rose and her new husband, Ted, who were honeymooning there. Ted would take me fishing for salmon by moonlight in Loch Fee, an unsportsmanlike sport in which you shone a torch on the water to attract a fish, whereupon you would give it a dirty great sock, gaff it and make for the shore. This was all very well when the lake was calm, but when a squall blew up it became a sea and then, all thoughts of fishing banished, we would paddle madly to shore.

In post-war Britain clothing was still on coupons. The black market was the order of the day, and Mummy was not immune from its temptations. While we were in Ireland she discovered that tweed was a quarter of its price in England; so she bought a length and, before our departure for home, wrapped it round her waist, then assumed a phantom pregnancy by putting on a maternity frock. I don't know what the customs officers thought as we passed through the 'Nothing to Declare' notice, but they let us through on the nod.

My second year at Cone-Ripman was also crowned with success when, jointly with Margaret Ann Wedlake, I won the coveted Drama Cup. But that wasn't all: the prize beyond rubies was a letter of introduction to the actor-director Robert Atkins, then the greatest provider of employment in the theatre – and this also I obtained. Thus armed, I was graciously received by the great man, auditioned successfully and, after negotiations conducted on my behalf by Sylvia Fisher, agent for the Arts Educational Schools, a weekly stipend of £4 was agreed upon. I then left the warm security of drama school to chance my arm in the professional theatre. I was a pro.

Not all that successful, though, at the start. There were many tricks of the trade I had still to learn – basic stage movements such as 'up R down L', for instance. It was ignorance of this that caused my downfall in the Regent's Park Open Air Theatre production of *Much Ado about Nothing*. When Robert instructed me to 'Go down R' I froze, thus fully deserving his 'Get off the bloody stage, Crowther!' a direction which still rings in my ears. So do the sniggers among the cast, though the kindlier ones drew me aside and instructed me in this and other mysteries.

Robert was very fond of canasta, which he played ad nauseam with his wife, Ethel, a pleasant enough lady who got on well with the company, especially its younger members. However, she had one disturbing habit: she rolled her own cigarettes with strong tobacco and the pungent fumes from these deposited a nicotine smudge between mouth and nose which in a lesser woman would have been offensive.

Robert, a professional to his fingertips, could follow a play instinctively, seemingly with half a mind. I have seen him rise from the canasta table with a muttered apology to Ethel, pick up his hat and walk on to the stage exactly on cue. But this didn't always work. I recall one occasion at the Open Air Theatre when we, the cast of *A Midsummer Night's Dream*, had repaired to the marquee ('The Tent') to avoid a sudden downpour, taking the audience with us as was the custom. We then realised that Robert was playing canasta in the wings by the open stage and as his entrance was coming up I, as the fleetest of foot, was despatched to apprise him of the situation. Unfortunately I thundered up the duckboards just too late to prevent Robert as Pyramus from declaiming to an empty auditorium:

> O grim-look'd night!
> O night with hue so black
> O Christ, where is everybody?

There are so many stories about Robert. Another in which I was involved again centred on a production of *A Midsummer Night's Dream*. This time it was Festival of Britain Year, 1951; Robert, as usual, played Pyramus, and I was cast as his lover Thisbe. In the 'play within a play', which the rude mechanicals put on to celebrate the nuptials of Theseus and Hippolyta, Robert had to commit a comic suicide, laying his massive frame centre stage after uttering his closing lines:

Tongue, lose thy light;
Moon, take thy flight.
Now die, die, die, die, die.

It was then my turn to come on and dance about behind his corpse, wringing my hands and declaiming before following him into eternal night. Unfortunately I overdid it. Having learned some aspects of Greek dance at the Cone-Ripman I proceeded to use it for comic effect. Borne along by the gusts of laughter from the auditorium, I carried on until I heard Robert growl: 'Stop buggering about.' Unfortunately the audience heard him too, loud and clear. He'd forgotten that the stage was equipped with a new Trix sound system and that he had collapsed next to the mike. Anyway, it cured me of indulging in too much 'business' – at least when on stage with Robert.

Not that I made many more appearances with his company. The time soon came when I had to look for a new job, a prospect which so many professional actors face with trepidation. But before leaving them I must mention a memorable occasion during the run of *A Midsummer Night's Dream* at the St Martin's Theatre, Drury Lane, in the winter of 1949. As ever I was playing Thisbe, and the entire cast were entranced by Jill Bennett's Titania. Whether the audience of infants were similarly carried away I doubt – they'd probably rather have been at a pantomime.

Anyway, it occurred to my Dad that we ought to throw a party for the cast. No sooner said than done: he at once proceeded to organise it and, knowing the propensity of all self-respecting pros to free-load when it came to food and drink, we did not stint on the victuals. A mutually convenient night was agreed, and all the cast promised to come over to Twickenham.

On the afternoon of the great day Dad and I were putting the finishing touches to the finger buffet while awaiting the arrival of our guests when there was an imperious knock on the door. I found Godfrey Tearle on the doorstep and as I stood there open-mouthed he enquired in mellifluous tones: 'Does Leslie Crowther live here?'

On my replying that I was indeed he, the great man intoned: 'Well, I've brought Jill Bennett to see you', and sure enough up the path walked Jill. They were living together at that time, he the patrician and very distinguished actor-manager of the old school, she an up-and-coming actress but by no means the star she was to become.

Declining the offer of a pre-prandial drink, he made off to keep a prior engagement – a party with Laurence Olivier – leaving Jill behind. It always impressed me that Jill had turned down a far more prestigious party for mine, simply because I'd invited her first. It spoke volumes for her integrity and loyalty.

One by one the rest of them arrived. Being in the same company meant that they were all on familiar terms, and the party went with a swing from the start. Dad was really enjoying himself, and when this was remarked on he replied that there was nothing he enjoyed more than the company of pros, because he'd been one himself. That did it! They insisted that he re-enact one of his variety turns, and this he did as the young pros lay draped on sofas and armchairs or spreadeagled on the floor. I was as enthralled as the rest of them while he set the scene, because it was as new to me as it was to them.

As he talked we could visualise him turning up at the variety theatre in whatever town he was appearing, with a painted backcloth representing a jungle scene and a papier mâché log. His costume would consist of a solar topee, and full tea planter's outfit including the inevitable long shorts. Oh yes, and his props would include a sari which was reserved for whichever local girl he could persuade to wear it. The girl would be either his landlady or her daughter, whom, as he quaintly put it, he would 'service' during his week's stay (he was a good-looking bloke, my Dad!). The chosen one would be clad in the sari, her unclothed parts rubbed liberally with burnt cork, and she would be taught to say, 'Tell me about England, *tuan*.'

This would be the cue for my father, by this time sitting on his papier mâché log, to doff his topee, wipe his moist brow, and, gazing into the front row of the dress circle as representing the middle distance, proceed to declaim:

74

It lay at the foot of the Chiltern Hills,
A hundred souls in all we were:
We had our church, our village green
And in the evening the happy laughter of village lads
Playing cricket could be heard, and their voices
Sounded very pleasant in the still night air.

The assembled company were hanging on his every word,
entranced. Meanwhile I was fumbling through my music titles
as I knew that the finale to his monologue would need an
accompaniment:

In the dear homeland, far across the sea
Did I wonder, do they ever think of me;
Do they sometimes long just to hold my hand,
Or perchance am I forgotten in my dear homeland?

Now Dad pulled his master stroke, doing an encore and
inviting them all to join in – and they all did, including Jill:

Did they sometimes long just to hold my hand,
Or perchance was I forgotten in that dear homeland?

Dear God! My Dad had never gone down so well. It was
probably the last chance he had to do his variety act – and
he hadn't even had to 'service' the landlady!

On the point of quitting Robert's company, I had a stroke
of luck. The Arts Educational Trust, in the lovely person of
Sylvia Fisher, the agent there, once more stepped in as my
fairy godmother. The Trust had for some time been supplying
the Festival Ballet with dancers for their corps de ballet, and
it so happened that at the crucial time for me they were stuck
for a mime artist to play Von Rothbart, the Owl Magician
and wicked uncle of Odette in *Swan Lake*. Sylvia, knowing of
my musical background and terpsichorean pretensions, offered
the job to me. So off I went, quitting the hairy-arsed company
of Shakespearian clowns for the sweaty fraternity of ballet

75

performers. I was thrilled to find that the principal dancers in *Swan Lake* were Alicia Markova as Odette and Anton Dolin as the Prince. Some responsibility for a novice – and I nearly ballsed it up on my first night!

It happened at the point in the ballet where I as Von Rothbart had to lure Odette away from the Prince, interrupting their *pas de deux*. No one had told me that my musical cue was the *reprise* of the passage of music in question. So when it played for the first time on to the boards I ponced, upstage of Markova and Dolin. The audience must have been puzzled to see a somewhat uncomfortable wicked uncle hovering in the backgroud, turning the passionate *pas de deux* into a *ménage à trois*. With consummate artistry Dolin, abandoning a surprised Markova, grand-jetéd sideways towards me, hissed, 'Get off the bloody stage', and rejoined his partner. Needing no second prompt, I fluttered off stage as I fondly imagined an owl would do, to find the corps de ballet splitting their tu-tus laughing – though they pulled themselves together in time to push me back on to the stage when my real cue came up.

Incidentally, it was Markova who revealed to me that even the most ethereal principal ballerina is only human. The orchestra for this production included a violinist who was consistently so pissed that Tchaikovsky must have curled up in his crypt at every performance. On one particular night Markova drifted towards me with her usual angelic smile, hissing, 'Listen to that bloody violin!'

All this time I was pursuing the lovely Somerset Jean, she of the lunch-queue leotard. At first I met with little success. She dubbed me 'the callow youth' and was more amused than bowled over by my ardour. But I had an ace up my sleeve. In a fit of wild extravagance my parents had bought a 1934 Ford 8 which, thanks to tuition patiently dispensed by 'Mickey', one of Mother's PGs, I had learned to drive. This mechanical love-aid greatly enhanced my chances of success and I regularly buzzed round to her digs with a bottle of cider secreted within my black duffle coat, like a caricature of the Sandeman's port advert.

Jean had a room in a sort of theatrical ladies' seminary

run by Mrs T. and Mrs D., who ran it rather on the lines of a high-security prison, though its forbidding aspect would usually be relieved by snatches of the piano part of a Beethoven concerto, the soaring notes of stringed instruments or the trilling of a female voice practising scales. Occasionally a flush-faced youth would emerge, as the place was a veritable honey-pot and the warders couldn't keep all the b——s out.

Then fortune dealt me a wonderful card. We were cast together as 'Jean and Leslie', an all-singing, comic, acting duo in the radio version of the *Ovaltineys Concert Party of the Air*, which was recorded at the Abbey Road studios in Maida Vale, home to the London Symphony Orchestra and, later, the Beatles. By this time my passion for Jean had reached the stage where I was investing vast sums in bunches of violets, which she accepted with embarrassed amusement.

We had great fun at Abbey Road. Clarence Wright was the producer – a wonderful man and one of the stalwarts of Tommy Handley's *ITMA*, the radio show which did so much to keep Britain laughing during the dark days of the war and in the post-war period of austerity. 'Always put a smile in your voice,' he would tell us. I still smile at the remembrance of his *ITMA* characters: 'Good morning, nice day' and 'Don't forget the diver.'

Jean and I shared many exciting adventures. On one occasion we went to a West End cinema in a typical London pea-souper, the fog so thick that it invaded the interior and we couldn't see the screen. We got a refund, of course, and returned on the tube to St John's Wood station. Walking from there to Jean's place turned my immaculate white shirt sulphur-yellow!

I was still keeping up my music, and at about this time I took part in a Junior Exhibitioners' concert at Duke's Hall. Jean came along and was suitably impressed by my masterly rendition of a Chopin *étude* which I'd memorised and managed not to forget.

Then we were again thrown together professionally – in a show for under twenty-ones, compèred by Michael Miles and called *Accent on Youth*. What a show! Among the cast were Julian Bream, Anthony Wager, Tony Newley, Shani Wallis,

Dilys Laye, Annie Hart (who later became Mrs Ronnie Corbett), Jean – and myself supplying the character voices. Noel Whitcomb, a *Daily Mirror* reporter, wrote an article about Dilys Laye and me saying that we were 'but two performers in a show bristling with talent only a taxi ride from the West End'.

In those days you didn't get the key to the door until you were twenty-one, but the powers-that-be anticipated the future by calling-up the nation's youth for National Service at the age of eighteen. You didn't get the vote, but you did get an official letter telling you to report at so-and-so to register.

Mother had made up her mind that my promising career should not be interrupted by a two-year break. Her experience in the theatre – and with Father – had taught her that once derailed it was often difficult to get back on track. She therefore begged me to register as a conscientious objector. This was a difficult decision for me. On the one hand I didn't want to dodge the column. On the other I was all too conscious of the debt I owed to Mother, who had sacrificed a lot to give me the chances she had never had.

In the end I did register, a decision I came to regret deeply. Looking back, I think this was when I really grew up – and started to lie. Whenever in conversation with my peers the question of National Service came up I would always fall back on the old excuse – medically unfit – as I had, after all, had TB meningitis. Thus far I'd taken things pretty much in my stride. Now I'd had a big decision to make and – as my conscience soon told me – I'd got it wrong.

Anyway, I duly appeared before a tribunal at Walham Green who excused me military duties but decreed that I must perform some kind of essential labour which, it was made clear to me, didn't include theatre. I was adjusting to this with youth's resilience when the unthinkable happened.

I was driving round London one morning in November 1951 with Mother when she complained of a nagging headache, which seemed to get worse. I stopped at the Regent's Palace Hotel for coffee, and while Mother went downstairs to the Ladies I had a quick haircut. After forty minutes she hadn't returned, so I went below to see what, if anything, was wrong. Peeping under the door, the female attendant saw that she had slumped to the floor, apparently unconscious.

We tried the door but it was locked. There was nothing for it: I had to climb in. Looking down, I saw to my horror that the left side of her body, including her face, was contorted. I knew enough to realise that she had suffered a massive stroke. She was rushed to the Charing Cross Hospital and Father was summoned to her bedside. But she never recovered – the stroke had been too serious. The unremitting struggle to keep the family together – early-morning insurance round, paying guests, turkey rearing; the long cycle ride to London; the problems posed by Father's drinking and her anxieties over my education and budding career – all had taken their toll. She was fifty-six years old, and I can truthfully say that hardly once during our eighteen years together did she ever slow down. Father took her death badly, haunted no doubt by feelings of guilt at his failings as a husband.

As for myself, after the initial surge of grief I was sustained by the thought that she had seen me take the first steps on the ladder of my chosen career, and had been particularly pleased with my success in *Accent on Youth*. I resolved there and then to carry on working for her sake. As it happened, I was under contract with the BBC Schools Service to do a broadcast that day and decided to go ahead with it, knowing it would have been her wish. So, leaving Pop to keep vigil at her bedside, I turned up at the studio.

George Dixon, the producer, noticed that something was wrong and asked what it was. Poor George! The very enquiry loosed all sorts of pent-up emotions and I broke down completely, sobbing uncontrollably in his arms. But that was the only time I allowed myself grief for the departure of my mother, because the show had to go on. All other feelings were kept bottled up – in my case a bottle of alcohol – and it was not until thirty-seven years later when I was asked to write a letter to my mother while at the Clouds Treatment Centre for alcoholism, that it all came pouring out to such an extent than it quite took me by surprise.

Darling Mummy

Since your sudden death, all those years ago, I have never written to thank you for your life. I know now what a tough and bitter life you must have led with Daddy. And lead you did. You had to. I remember the extra work you took on in Nottingham and Twickenham to make the extra money to give me a good education, and then drama school. I remember the cycle ride you and I did to London and the way you organised our stay on the Isle of Bute, when the flying bomb nearly killed us both in Richmond. Sticking a pin in a Scottish telephone directory, taking the name and address where the pin landed, and persuading the evacuation authorities that you knew the people, and that they should pay our fare to be evacuated away from the buzz bomb target area was something only you would have done. Everyone, including the Scottish farmer who took us in for the duration of the war with Germany, recognised you for the courageous and wonderful woman you are. Only I know how painful and dreary your life really was most of the time. The screaming matches, the financial struggles, the scheming to make ends meet, and the way you always tried to look presentable on school open days, and drama school productions, were a tribute to your love and dedication. All of it focused on me. I feel ashamed that I was embarrassed when you turned up looking careworn and slightly shabby, when you had gone to such efforts to look good. I remember the good things, too. The picnics during the war in the meadow by the River Trent, the visits to the West End Theatre in 1946 when I saw the Old Vic Company, and my first spectacular musical production at the Coliseum. Do you remember the gallery queues and the buskers who entertained us as we waited in the freezing cold? The visits to the museums and art galleries? The pantomimes at the Theatre Royal in Nottingham during the war, especially the one where Dad got up on stage? The audience laughed and laughed, and I was so proud of him. Then I turned to share my pride with you, and you were crying. I didn't really know why then, but I do now. All those memories of the handsome actor you fell in love with must have welled up inside you, and your heart must have been breaking.

Had you lived, you would have seen your son going the same way. Luckily I have – with God's grace and help – arrested the problem that I failed to understand in Daddy. Rather I have begun to arrest it. I only wish you had known about the disease of alcoholism. You would have understood him better. He was as bitter and disillusioned as you were, and he never knew why.

Dearest Mummy, I forgive you for making me become a conscientious objector. I hadn't the courage to stand up to you at the age of eighteen, and when you were being as strong as you could so often be, you intimidated me. I was actually frightened of you at times; did you know that? My God, I loved you though. When you died, my world collapsed for a day, and then I braced myself to do you proud. I analysed at the time whether I was grieving for you enough – I can actually remember doing that – and, of course, I wasn't. As you know, I was going steady with Jean by then, and I think you were afraid that she was going to take me away from you. She was certainly afraid of you, but has now grown to appreciate what an indomitable and caring woman you are.

Honesty is the name in this programme at Clouds House, where I am being treated for alcoholism. Yes, the same disease your husband died of. Honesty means that I can tell you feelings I have for you that I have never dared tell you before. Of course I loved you, but there were times when I felt controlled by you, cowed by you, angry with you, resentful towards you, wary of you, and, when you made more demands of me than I could meet, I hated you. It was a passing, petty hatred, but I didn't like the feeling.

You know, however, exactly how much I loved you. I

often felt immensely sorry for you, and the way you had to cope with Daddy's unreasoning rages. I hated to see you crying so bitterly after each blazing row. The strong, reassuring mother became so vulnerable. You would hug me and hug me, and Daddy would go away.

Wherever you are, Mummy, and I know you're somewhere with God, I hope you are at peace. Your body looked very peaceful when I kissed you goodbye.

With my love and gratitude for all you endeavoured to do for me – and this time I will live up to your dreams.

Your son – Leslie.

Still the prey of confused feelings soon after my mother's death, I then called on Jean and blurted out that I had got to dedicate myself to my career and that we must never see each other again. I shall always carry the vision of her slight figure in the doorway and the expression of hurt surprise as she received this outburst. It was difficult not to see each other since we were working together the following week in *Accent on Youth*. Thank God I later recovered my senses, and we fell in love all over again.

Someone asked me recently what it was that first attracted me to Jean. Had I but known prior to my wedding day that there were such gifts of loyalty, honesty, compassion, and love all included in that tiny frame I would never have dared to propose to her, for the simple reason that I haven't the capacity to equal those talents, match for match. Come to think of it, I didn't propose to her, she proposed to me. Or at least she made me propose to her. Quite the most sensible thing I've ever done. And in the last forty years I've had to stand in wonderment at all the aforesaid attributes. Were I but to make a list of all her assets nobody would believe me, that is unless you were married to her yourself. Then you'd find out. The only thing I've contributed to her in the way of assets is money. Would to God I could have contributed more. What is money, after all? I have learnt honesty and compassion from her, and received masses of love.

But in the meantime the gap left by Mother's death and the

worry of what to do about Father and keeping the house going, together with the pressures exerted by my acting commitments, were literally driving me to drink. The growing fear that I might be destined to follow the same downward path as Father made matters worse. Nevertheless we *did* have to keep going, and we decided to convert the PGs' rooms into bed-sitters; meters were installed for their gas fires and rings, and they dealt with their own cooking.

That autumn the hugely popular singer Dorothy Squires was holding auditions for the double part of Alderman Fitzwarren/Sultan of Morocco in *Dick Whittington and His Cat*, which was due to open at the New Cross Empire on 22 December 1951. I went along and got the part. The pantomime was hugely successful, and Dorothy's personality endeared her to the audiences. At that time she was having a ding dong with Roger Moore. I must say I was impressed whenever he came to the stage door. He was a star in the J. Arthur Rank chain of featured artists – and, of course, exceedingly handsome. *Dick Whittington* unfortunately lasted only a month and then, like Christmas, we closed.

To add to my worries the bogey of 'essential labour' imposed by the tribunal reared its head, just as I was getting into my stride in 1952 in a show entitled *Intimacy at Eight* at the New Lindsay Theatre, Notting Hill Gate. Written by Peter Myers and Alec Grahame, who had collaborated so brilliantly to create *Accent on Youth*, and with music by Ronnie Cass, the show had a splendid cast including Dilys Laye, Ron Moody, Eunice Gayson, Joan Sims and Peter Felgate – and I was chosen as lynchpin.

The daytime job I landed was as a baker's roundsman, and it was then that I really learned the meaning of 'resilience'. Not that I felt particularly resilient getting up at 5.30 after giving my all the night before. And it was a long day. Up and down paths to houses and in and out of blocks of flats I darted, delivering the staff of life. Often after a long ascent to a top-floor flat I would find a note requesting a different-shaped loaf, and down the stairs I would have to clatter before making a much slower reascent. After a day doing that I would be absolutely knackered, but that wasn't all. On the return round I had to get the money out of them. All in all it would be about 4.30 before I finished, when I would crawl into bed, relying on Father to wake me up in time to get to the theatre promptly at 7.25 p.m.

As for rehearsals, I was more often than not conspicuous by my absence, but no one seemed put out by this and as usual youthful resilience carried me through. Anyway, I managed to keep the candle burning at both ends, and indeed the show burned so brightly that, under its new title *High Spirits*, it transferred to the Hippodrome in the West End where it opened on 13 May 1953 and played for three months.

My career as a baker's roundsman didn't last long, and as the powers-that-be failed to notice its demise I was able to fit in a nice little tour with *High Spirits* before we opened at the Hippo. And open we did with a cast led by Cyril Richard, Diana Churchill and Ian Carmichael, backed up by Patrick Cargill, Ron Moody, Dilys Laye, Thelma Ruby, Ronnie Stevens, Eleanor Fazan, Maxwell Coker, Marie Bryant – and me. With a cast like that, could it have been other than a smash success?

Unfortunately its success woke up the Ministry of Labour to the hiatus in the 'essential work' obligation imposed by the tribunal as an alternative to military service. They directed me to the geriatric ward of the South Western Fever Hospital run by one Sister Trollope, who belied her name by turning out to be a tartar. More than that I cannot say, as I believe she is still alive and living in Devon, but if she ever ventures our way I shall break out in beads of sweat and run for cover!

But there's always a silver lining. The SRN on the ward, John Bennett, took me under his wing and in no time at all had brought me to the high state of efficiency in bedmaking which I have maintained to this day, though in the weeks following my accident I was more made against than making.

Apart from bedmaking, my job as ward orderly entailed wheeling patients to the sluice, giving them bed baths, feeding them when necessary and ministering to whatever other needs they had. One of the most frequent needs involved use of the bedpan, and this essential item featured in a little cameo towards the end of my first day in the ward, when Matron swept in to see how I was getting on.

I had just given one of my patients a bedpan, accompanied by a chipped enamel bowl containing tow, or cotton waste, which in those days of post-war austerity was used as a cheap substitute for toilet paper. It looked like desiccated candy floss but served its purpose reasonably well.

'Well, young man, how are you getting on?' Matron asked, pausing at my bedspace.

'Fine, Matron,' I replied with an air of authority as if in complete control. 'I've just screened this patient off. Everything is in order.'

Just then the old guy yelled from behind the screen, 'I've finished!' To which I replied, summoning up my one-day's nursing knowledge, 'Well, use your tow.'

His response was immediate. 'What do you think I am – a bloody contortionist?' Alas, the English language has ever been a vehicle for hilarious misunderstandings.

It was hard work but there was a lot of fun too, and I had the satisfaction of knowing that I was serving others. So when it suddenly came to an end I felt at a bit of a loss. Not for long, though. After *High Spirits* closed in the autumn of 1953 I was fortunate when Frederic Piffard employed me as juvenile character man at the Richmond Repertory Company. It was there that I first worked with an actor called Peter Hughes. Dear God, we were twin souls, comedywise – we both had the same giggly sense of humour. In fact many's the time the dramatic action of the play slowed down or even collapsed completely due to an insane fit of giggles brought on by Pete and me. By gum, we positively choked such was our desire to control ourselves. Luckily we were firm favourites with our audience, who tolerated it. Incidentally, a firm favourite in rep is one whose first entrance in a piece is greeted with rapturous applause.

Anyway, an actor and I were waiting for our entrance during the rehearsal for the next week's offering when he asked me out of the blue how old I was. 'I shall be 21 on 6 February,' I said.

'Happy birthday,' he replied. 'It's 6 February.'

We repaired to the Cobwebs, the local hostelry, and celebrated in as much style as we could muster.

At Richmond, in the Christmas 1953 season I had played Idle Jack in my second pantomime (my first having been at New Cross in 1951). I was now busying myself being non-idle Les in preparation for my marriage to Jean.

In the cast of *Intimacy at Eight* the previous year at the New Lindsay Theatre was Peter Felgate, whose talents were equalled by his godfather, Greatrex Newman. Greatrex wrote for and ran the Fol-de-Rols, a relic of the classic seaside concert party but still alive and kicking and billed as 'The only show a child could take its parents to'. It was really intimate revue under another name, with the bonus of sand and sea. By great good fortune Greatrex, known to all as Rex, had come to see *Intimacy* on a particularly good night for me and promptly offered me a job with the Fol-de-Rols whenever I wanted one. Spurred on by this I got in touch with Jean and offered her a job – marriage to me for life – which, I'm pleased to say, she accepted with alacrity.

From then on we were frantically busy. On her death, Mummy had left the house to me, not my Dad, and he duly appointed himself regent; but such was his muddled approach to his care coupled with his drinking habits that in my twenty-first birthday he bequeathed me a sheaf of bills from the electricity, water and gas boards and for the rates – plus the little matter of the mortgage. In those days you didn't come of age until your twenty-first birthday but, by golly, that was enough to put years on me.

We resolved to take over the ground floor of Number 225 as a flat for ourselves, and remove one of the tenants from an upstairs room and install Dad in it. With a bit of painting and decorating we made our new home as pleasant as possible until we came to the cooker, which was unusable. 'You leave and sort out the wedding day,' I said to Jean, 'and I'll deal with the cooker. See you in Keynsham.'

Thus it was that, the night before the wedding, Jean and her doubting Daddy were waiting on Number 1 platform at Bath Station for my arrival. But I didn't turn up! Hearts fluttered, and her father was just about to say 'I told you so', when it occurred to him to check on the arrival time of the next train from London. He was told that this was in half an hour, and they waited. It duly sailed in with me on it: sighs of relief all round.

I put the whole blame for my non-arrival on the cooker. The dirt just wouldn't budge. Something else that wouldn't shift were the holes in the soles of my shoes. Realising that these would be revealed as we knelt down in front of the congregation I explained the situation to Jean's father, who offered to drive me into Keynsham the next morning to purchase a new pair. Little point in telling him that his future son-in-law was boracic lint (skint) – that would immediately have brought the rejoinder 'I *told* you so.' So I resolved the situation by polishing the soles black to match my socks.

Fol-de-Rols

We were married at St John the Baptist's church, Keynsham – Jean's home ground in the West Country – on Saturday, 27 March 1954. The bill for our one-night stay at the Swan Hotel, Wells, was settled with a welcome cheque from Jean's Uncle Bill which had been intended for the purchase of a blanket – to this day unbought. Then it was back on the train to 225 Richmond Road, Twickenham, with Father in tow, to start married life together.

Newly wedded bliss was cut short by my having to rise at the crack of dawn to attend rehearsals for the Fols, which took place in the heart of London. Here we knocked off the two out of three programmes required if we were going to open in Summer Season. The bill of fare changed every Thursday, so that punters spending a fortnight by the sea who turned up and liked the first offering could fit in two more visits during their stay without seeing hysteria repeating itself.

I turned up for that first rehearsal with butterflies in my stomach at the prospect of venturing into the new world of variety – a cruel one, as I knew from Father's experience and from what I'd gleaned from other pros. Strange, isn't it? Here was I, just out of an intimate revue regarded by most variety pros as brilliant and the best of its kind, experiencing colly-wobbles at the thought of joining what most people would have considered a less daunting line of variety. Perhaps it was my new-found sense of responsibility as a married man, or the realisation that on my initial impact might hang the prospect of reasonably permanent employment – that actor's vision which so often turns out to be a mirage!

To some extent my fears were justified. Jack Tripp, another

newcomer to the Fols, was nearly my downfall. I could certainly
have done without him. He'd brought along several hilarious
sketches which one could see would raise peals of laughter, and
to add insult to injury he could tap dance like Jack Buchanan.
On top of all this he did a hysterical 'ballet' with the girls, while
I was fobbed off with a character sketch. Consequently I went
home that night to a new wife feeling most unhappy, in spite of
the fact that Kathleen West, the comedienne, had recognised
what was going on and had done her best to jolly me along.

But all thoughts of 'poor me' evaporated on the first night,
and every night thereafter – blown away by the speed of the
quick changes. Oh, those quick changes! When I first put on
the traditional opening costume I found that the outfitters had
made it two sizes too large. I soon discovered why. Beneath
the top layer went different costumes for at least the two
following scenes. As the layers peeled off like onion skins
we not only grew cooler but knew that the programme was
half over!

The Fols tradition was that after rehearsals were over the
show would go on tour for six weeks or so to various seaside
resorts before settling down at the Summer Season venue.
Programme number three would be rehearsed in the daytime
during the tour. 'Trying it out on the dog', it was called – a Rex
Newmanism which I always thought rather callous, bearing in
mind that the 'dogs' had paid their hard-earned money at the
box office.

That first summer we settled down at the Pavilion, Torquay
and it was like a honeymoon – in fact it *was* our honeymoon and
I got paid for it! As I got slimmer with the quick changes Jean
got fatter, because she was pregnant. My agent had booked me
for pantomime in Leeds that Christmas and asked if Jean would
like to be in the show, too. 'Only if it's *Humpty Dumpty*,' I
replied. The prospect of fatherhood was rather daunting. Jean
was to have the baby in Twickenham, and then when it was big
enough would join me in Leeds.

At the end of the Torquay season, we returned to Twickenham
and one Sunday evening went to church where the vicar, the
Reverend Wilfred Burton, pulled one of his best gaffes. After
the service Wilfred stood at the church doorway – as he had

done on countless Sundays before – saying goodbye and even muttering a few extra words (we always said he was counting the house) to those he knew. He knew us well and was aware that we'd been away in Summer Season. As Jean hove into sight she looked for all the world like a galleon in full sail, being seven months pregnant. He took one look at her and said: 'Well, well, and how are we? Full of beans?' Not a surprising remark, really, for a man whose contribution to the church magazine had once been: 'Your prayers are entreated for George Johnson, who is lying in the West Middlesex Hospital calmly and courageously holding his own.'

We were looking forward to the baby's birth, which was due on Christmas Day. In those days, if you were 'on the Health' you were obliged to allow your body to become a living specimen for the instruction of would-be doctors and surgeons. The film *Doctor in the House* featured just such a scene. On one visit to the ante-natal clinic the James Robertson Justice character duly arrived at Jean's bedside surrounded by his student band and asked one of them to examine her. After applying his stethoscope to the vital spot he straightened up and said: 'Well, I am definitely hearing another heartbeat.'

'Nonsense!' boomed the specialist. 'It's a single birth.' But the student stood his ground so firmly that the great man himself gave Jean the once-over. 'My God,' he conceded. 'You're right – it's multiple.' I hope the lad made it to Harley Street.

When I swanned in at about 8.30 that night I was given the order: 'Twin pram, double quantity of Harrington Squares . . . double everything!'

The nurse who accompanied the ambulance which took Jean to the West Middlesex Hospital was a cool number. Jean, naturally wishing to share her excitement, exclaimed: 'I'm having twins!'

'I know,' came the level reply. 'If you think for one minute that I'm in the habit of leaving the hospital without studying my patient's case history. . . .' The rest went unsaid, but she hadn't finished. Turning to me as I was about to climb in to go with Jean she said, as if I had crawled out from under a stone: 'We shan't need you.'

The twins duly and safely arrived and were placed in separate cots. On my first visit, Lindsay was crying. 'Why is she doing that?' I asked.

'It's a healthy sign,' the nurse replied.

'Then why isn't the other one doing it?'

I don't recall the answer to this penetrating paternal probe.

Whilst there I witnessed for the first time that amazing spectacle – the double-breasted milk-feed. The sight of the two *enfants terribles* suckling away, cradled in Jean's arms, is one I shall never forget.

Thank God it *was* twins! Jean had been due to give birth nine months to the day after our wedding but they arrived two weeks early, on 9 December 1954 – and I had to leave for panto in Leeds on the 11th. An early birth is, of course, a normal occurrence with twins. Had it been a single blessing Jean's mother would have thought it suspicious, convinced as she was that we had been at it before the nuptials.

While I was in Leeds with the panto Jean's Mum came up to Twickenham to be with her during my absence. She stayed for the whole of the run, bless her soul, and even for a while after my return. Indeed she seemed reluctant to leave, even after my return. As I made my re-entry clutching milk bottles she happened to ask; 'Is it cold out?' to which I replied 'It's so cold out I've put it back.' Her indignant squawk, followed by ribald laughter, told me that I'd struck home.

Jean was in her seventh heaven then. Not only did she have her Mum's pair of hands to help cope with the twins, but mine as well. Mind you, I'm not sure mine were always useful, and certainly on one occasion they were otherwise engaged at a moment of particular crisis.

This was when the twins had to be presented at the hospital for an MOT. While Jean was dressing them I sat at the piano practising, oblivious to the fact that Liz, all dressed and ready for the road, was doing a poo. Jean tried to attract my attention, but to no avail. So, covered in poo handwise, she proceeded to bang on the newly decorated wall. When I saw the marks on the paintwork it was my turn to bang on – which I did boringly on that and other occasions.

Later I became a much more 'hands-on' Daddy as Jean rather kindly puts it, and I have enjoyed fatherhood – and grandfatherhood. Which is just as well, having at the time of writing five children of my own and twelve grandchildren.

I remember the opening of that panto season in Leeds as idyllic, perhaps because it was my first as a fully fledged pro. It wasn't my actual first: that had been *Robinson Crusoe* in 1951 at the New Cross Empire, followed two years later by *Dick Whittington* at Richmond Rep – where my love affair with pantomime had really begun. But my role as Abanazar in the Leeds *Aladdin* was the real thing and confirmed the panto passion which, with appropriate gaps when other work intervened, has been lifelong.

But the idyll didn't last long. As so often in my career, reality broke through to remind me that life beyond the footlights could be cruel.

We played *Aladdin* on Christmas Eve, which was when Jean took the twins home from hospital, so after the show I caught the night train to London. Arriving on the doorstep at Twickenham at 8 a.m. I learned from Jean that Father was in hospital, having been involved in a bad accident. Apparently he'd nipped down to the corner pub to celebrate the twins' arrival, taking the dog. On emerging, the dog had slipped his lead and darted across the road. Ill-advisedly, because the pub was on a blind corner, Pop had made chase and collided with a car.

I was soon at his bedside at the West Middlesex – the same hospital in which the twins had so recently been born. There he lay, all bruised and broken, but conscious. He kept repeating, 'I saw the twins.' Jean told me that when she'd reached home from hospital Pop's face had been one big smile of welcome. He died ten days later, aged sixty-seven. My feelings about his death were very mixed. After Jean and I were married he had been a constant source of worry and expense. Though he paid no rent and we gave him a small allowance to supplement his pension, he had written to his sister telling her he needed a £12 radio and that we had refused to help him get one. She sent him the money thinking us very unfeeling, and unaware that he already had a set. We only learnt of this at his funeral. At that time I had no knowledge of the illness of alcoholism and felt relief that on his death he had been freed of his own personal hell, and, terrible though it may sound, I was glad he was out of our way. Again it was only when I went to Clouds and wrote a letter to him that I was able to truly forgive him.

'The show must go on' is a hackneyed phrase which Noël Coward satirically turned on its head in his '*Why* must the show go on?' But it is none the less a theatrical imperative – and never more so than in pantomime where the punters, who include a high proportion of children, are all looking forward to that annual treat without which no Christmas season would be complete. So six days after Father's funeral it was back to Leeds and *Aladdin* – putting a brave face on it, as they say, Mind you, my face nearly slipped when Denis Noble, the elderly and distinguished baritone playing the Emperor, with the best of intentions, pressed my hand gently and murmured 'Good luck, mate' as I stood in the wings ready to make my entrance after returning from Twickenham. The trouble he took to make sure that I was not alone moved me very much.

Looking back, I can see it was a godsend. Whatever your personal problems, you have to give your all on stage and the commitment required in pantomime is total. Altogether I've done eighteen – small beer when set against the numbers clocked up by other variety performers, but I treasure the memory of every one. Love it you had to – at twice daily it would otherwise have been just hard graft.

Before tripping back into another Fol-de-Rol season (and there were plenty more to come), perhaps a few peeps behind the panto proscenium might be in order. The day would start moving at about 9.30 when I would get up. Then at about ten I would start work. The first thing I'd do if away from home would be to ring Jean and see how she and the children were coping. Next I would answer letters, telephone my agent (*most* important) and then – almost as important – visit the antique shops. Since we had taken over a Victorian house Jean and I thought we'd fill the walls and floor with Victorian antiques. The decision was lucky in that Victoriana was largely denigrated in those days so we could pick things up for a song. Finally I would clock in at the theatre, usually at 1.25 p.m., ready for the matinée.

When you were on you were on. But any time not spent in the lawful pursuit of earning money on stage could be pleasantly passed in visiting other dressing rooms for useful chats, which would be interrupted frequently by the tannoyed tones of the stage manager summoning his troops into the firing line.

After the evening show it was time for bed. This could be in 'digs'; or, if you were lucky, at home; or, if you were considerably lucky, at the Nuneaton home of Abe Ball, an antiques buff of blessed acquaintance who, with his wife Ciss, always played host to me when I was appearing in Birmingham. Though permanently baffled by the vagaries of showbusiness, they could always be relied on to make me comfortable.

But back to the early stages of my passion for panto – Christmas 1954 and *Aladdin* at the Empire Theatre, Leeds, starring Nat 'Rubber Neck' Jackley, Jimmy Clitheroe and Denis Noble playing respectively the Widow Twankey, her son Wishee Washee and the Emperor of China. Apart from playing the wicked uncle Abanazar I also understudied the widow Nat.

The young lady playing Aladdin was Gillian Comber, who came fresh from *Daddy Long Legs* in the West End. Gill had been a member of the *Ovaltineys Concert Party of the Air* with Jean and me, so we knew each other. I must say it seemed a crying shame to be playing her wicked uncle! But needs must when the contract demands. A delightful young woman and, as every young man who had the hots for her can testify, extremely lovely, she joined me later in *Crackerjack*. Jean and I are still great friends with her.

We stayed – and I say 'we' because I shared digs with a winsome lass playing Princess Balroubadour – at Harehills Avenue with a Mrs Cowans, her daughter Marie and son Mike, who was later to be employed as a useful fast bowler by the Yorkshire County Cricket Club. The digs were also shared with hundreds of cats. I can't recall cats on the rooftops but I can still taste their hairs on the bacon and in the soup – and I swear that on one occasion I decapitated a boiled egg and found a cat's hair inside.

But while life there was rather hairy it was also comfortable. It was a pig of a winter, with the city mantled in frozen snow, so it was a treat to arrive at Harehills Avenue to find a freshly lit coal fire in the bedroom grate with ample stocks of fuel. Warmed by that and a well-stocked tray of provisions we were in clover, and could cheerfully put up with the hirsute moggies.

The following year, 1955, we played Hanley, Stoke-on-Trent and I actually got to play Widow Twankey – Nat Jackley had developed a painful bum-boil which rendered him *hors de combat*. I was hastily taught the trap routine in the bed-sit before debouching on to the stage. This involved lying on the upper deck of a double-decker bunk bed, and, on one, slipping the catch and, tucking myself in elbowwise, falling through to the lower bed to the accompaniment of wild hysteria from the audience and everyone else on stage. I can remember feeling very cool, but then I had the superb professionalism of Jimmy Clitheroe and Jack and Mannie Francois to pull me through. I actually enjoyed it.

That year Jean and the twins, who were just one, joined me and on this occasion we enjoyed our digs in Basford, at the home of the Collinses. This wonderful Jewish family, consisting of Robert and his beautiful daughter Miriam, were often joined by Robert's brother Guthrie, a teacher of art, and his sister, a music teacher, for musical soirées on Sunday evenings. The whole place was an artistic oasis. We still have Guthrie's ceramic figure of a miner – a true memento of this kindly Potteries family.

One of the twins, Lindsay, succumbed to the dreaded flu virus while we were there, a consequence no doubt of the arctic conditions. The season ended as she recovered from that, whereupon we subjected them both to a journey from Stoke-on-Trent to Twickenham via a snow-bound scenic route. The trip was made in a Hillman station wagon which I'd rashly bought and which let in blasts of cold air at every twist and turn.

Oh, the joy of sliding down Kenilworth High Street in the snowdrifts! It was a miracle that we managed to avoid cannoning into the shop fronts or parked cars, but miss them we did and drifted out of the town on to terra firma, and so to London, Twickenham and home. It was an eerie drive and I'll never forget approaching our house through row upon row of streets which, normally bustling, now stood silent, white and empty.

After Hanley, fifteen years were to pass before I got back into pantomime – busy and on the whole professionally successful years which simply ruled out the panto option. Mind you, when I did effect re-entry it was with a splash – at the Palladium with Cilla Black. But that's for later. Meanwhile, back to 1955 and my second season with the Fol-de-Rols.

Throughout my time with the Fols, 1954–9, the pace varied between breathless and hectic, and when not on stage we were on the road. In the spring of 1955 we even got as far as West Germany after Rex Newman had persuaded CSEU (the Combined Services Entertainment Unit, successor to ENSA) that the Fol-de-Rols would be an ideal fill-in, varietywise, for the star-studded cast which had been assembled.

How wrong he was! From the moment the curtain went up revealing the Fols company – the women in poke bonnets and crinolines, the men in beaver hats, velvet tails and figured waistcoats, all singing 'Come along and play with us'. . . . Well, we never got beyond that line. The squaddies in the audience let fly – no cast ever received such a barracking! We then proceeded to our ultimate and unscheduled performance in a nearby USAAF base, where we were treated with the utmost respect – such as the show deserved! The civility of the Americans, who in time-honoured fashion opened their fridges, was in sharp contrast to the reception by our own countrymen.

Our hosts had loaded the table with goodly fare, but as he led us to the dining hall the commanding officer said: 'If only we'd known, we'd have been prepared. I guess you'll have to make do with what we've managed to drag out of the deep freeze.' Lo and behold! There before our rationed eyes were sides of beef, hams, whole salmon, salads galore and sweets to make your mouth water. This one night of American hospitality was ample compensation for all the barracking that had gone before.

On our return journey to England George Hancock, the baritone in the show, said, 'There'll be no trouble at the customs, lads – the officer's one of our local Rotarians. I've written to him, and this morning I got a letter back assuring all of us a free passage.'

Unfortunately George was a line-shooter, and as a result nobody believed him. Well, we were all preparing to disembark when a voice called out: 'Mr George Hancock's party, proceed at once to the Customs Hall, please.' All of us knew that we'd made yet another mistake. If you're reading this, George – and if not, why aren't you? – a sincere apology from one of your doubting Thomases.

Every summer we would tour the seaside resorts of the British Isles. We played for two weeks the Connaught Theatre at Worthing, the White Rock Pavilion at Hastings and then on to the Winter Gardens in Margate before settling down for the season at the Pavilion Torquay or the Floral Hall, Scarborough.

Oh dear, the Floral Hall! I can still hear the din of the rain hitting the glass roof on nights when it chucked it down – a continuous sound I was not unaware of, since downpours in my days at the Open Air Theatre in Regent's Park made a similar noise on the marquee roof, drowning out any attempts at comic innuendo. Of course, this usually happened when someone important whom one was trying to impress was sitting out front.

We also toured Scotland in the winter, playing Edinburgh, Aberdeen and Glasgow. So the touring year was a full one, for which I was grateful as we had to keep the Twickenham house going and the regular income kept the red notices from gas, electricity and water boards – 'gypsy's warnings', in Father's parlance – at bay. Even so, it was a struggle. In taking over the house I'd also taken over the debts run up by Father, and quite considerable they were! Knocking them off left a gaping hole in the bank balance and we always started the following season in debt, which was rather painful.

We were also progressively emptying the rooms of tenants. The last two to leave were the Nunns, Rita and Charlie, who at the weekend often used to come in rather the worse for drink. When we were at home during rehearsal time we'd sometimes have to haul Rita upstairs to her room. Someone in the Fols said to me: 'You don't look very well. Sleepless night?'

My answer: 'Well, the Nunns came in drunk last night', rather took them aback, and I could see them summoning up a picture of several ladies wearing the habit indulging their habit again.

With the tenants gone, we filled the rooms with our children. Lindsay Jane and Elizabeth Ann, born in 1954, were followed by Caroline Susan who, born on 29 December 1958 in Edinburgh, was our only Scots bairn. Caroline was always very positive about her Scottishness. Once when the twins were being especially nauseating to her she burst out with remarkable flair: 'Anyway I'm Scottish, and when I grow up that's what I shall speak and you won't understand me.'

In this way the years slipped by. In retrospect they were carefree years, despite the difficulties of making ends meet, always with lots of fun – company outings, picnics and parties to relieve the hard work of touring and performing. On some of the darker days after I'd left them in 1960 I would look back on the Fol-de-Rol times with real nostalgia. Tom Mennard, for instance, a North Country comic, would lead a string of us in our cars on what he was pleased to call a mystery tour. When asked after a double circuit of the nearest roundabout where we were headed for he would invariably reply, 'I don't know, luv, that's the bloody mystery', whereupon we would pull into the nearest hostelry and laugh the night away.

Then there were those ridiculous last nights when at the curtain call farewell gifts would pile up in pyramids around us, brought up to the stage by the programme girls. Some of the bulkier ones we would have bought ourselves just in case there were not enough genuine ones to impress the audience. On one particular night at Scarborough the parting gifts included a bloody hare which turned out to have been bagged by Fred Trueman, who was appearing in the cricket festival there. He must have thought it an ideal last night gift, totally forgetting – if indeed he knew – that we were opening at the Lyceum, Edinburgh, the following Monday. If Fred is reading this I know he'll understand why we felt it best to donate it to a grateful butcher. Which provides my cue to call 'over' and indulge in a little cricketing reminiscence.

It was a cricketing sketch which drew me to Fred Trueman's attention when the Fol-de-Rols were in residence at Scarborough during the annual cricket festival week in 1957. My act was a solo in which I mimed, to the tune 'Shepherd's Hey', a batsman facing a Trueman-type fast bowler. As the audience invariably included a contingent of cricket festival-goers it raised plenty of laughs.

At this particular performance Fred, who had seen and enjoyed the sketch, came bounding into the dressing room and invited – nay, ordered – me to join him at the Balmoral Hotel (known, inevitably, as the Immoral) just as soon as I'd finished the show. Excited at the prospect of meeting some of my cricketing heroes, and with Jean on my arm, I duly turned up and was not disappointed. Fred was at the bar with Godfrey Evans and Johnny Wardle, and while Mrs Wardle made Jean feel at home I got on wi' t'lads. I'll never forget the manner of Godfrey Evans' leave-taking. He bid us 'Goodnight', was swallowed by the revolving doors and instantly regurgitated, when he fell upon us as if we were long-lost friends. Someone graciously pointed him to the hinged door alongside and he made a successful second exit, followed soon after and none too steadily by Jean and myself.

It was Jean's suggestion the next morning that I call at the North Parade cricket ground with a thank you bottle for Fred. This I did, to find that he had bowled ten overs at great pace, taken three wickets and seemed to have suffered no after-effects from the sixteen pints or so of Tetley's bitter which he'd put away. So had I, but there the resemblance ended. I felt awful.

Lest it be thought that I only *drank* with cricketers I would like to make it clear that I was a keen player and had been since boyhood.

When we started making the winter tour of Scotland with the Fol-de-Rols in 1956 we always spent Christmas in Auld Reekie. I well remember – how can I ever forget? – our first visit, which started immediately after the Scarborough season in 1955.

Jean and I had got fixed up with digs in Leith, the seaside port of Edinburgh. Our rooms were, to say the least, scantily furnished. There were no beds for the twins, and they couldn't even sleep in their pram because it had somehow got left behind on York Station when the company had changed trains. Jean had to use two drawers from the chest instead. Worse than this was the fact that the previous occupants had generously bequeathed us fleas, which we became aware of when Jean complained that she had come up in spots of the itching variety. 'Heat bumps,' I volunteered hopefully, ignoring the fact that it was twenty below – inside. It wasn't until the first little monster leaped across our startled gaze that we realised the true cause. It wasn't too bad, though, as we were only there for five weeks on that occasion. When the time came round for another stay in Edinburgh we decided to go upmarket – in Portobello.

The arrangement in the new digs was that we – Jean, self, twins and Hildegarde, the German au-pair we had taken on – should share house and kitchen with the landlady. As it turned out we also shared the traumas, because no sooner had we booked in than the landlady went mad. Our first intimation of this was when she wandered unexpectedly into the sitting room and let out a piercing scream, which elicited a '*Lieber Gott*!' from Hildegarde and mirth from the twins.

Poor dear. It turned out that her husband, a golf pro, had years ago taken unto himself a mistress with a penchant for French perfume and whenever he returned redolent of Chanel, it was more than his poor wife could take. After he'd left her the perfume, as it were, lingered on – she was haunted by a smell!

'Can you smell the gases?' she would ask. If one politely asked where she thought they were coming from, she would reply: '*They're* sending them.' This terrified the twins and I had to ask her to desist. After that, the minute she felt 'the gases' coming on she would climb out of the window and scream her heart out. She didn't want to disturb us, but the poor neighbours got the full blast. It was they who in the end alerted the health authorities and, sure enough, two men in white coats came to take her away. And do you know, as the poor woman was leaving she paused to apologise for having caused us inconvenience.

That was sad enough, but soon after we had recovered and moved on to Aberdeen the woman proprietor in the hotel next door to our digs went dotty and had to be removed by police and a fire engine! My fellow Fols found the propensity of the Crowthers to bring out latent dottiness in the local population highly amusing. As for Hildegarde, her '*Lieber Gotts*' became more and more guttural.

Scotland, however, got its own back on the Sassenachs in the shape of the landlady at our digs in Hill Street, Glasgow, then a slum area behind Sauchiehall Street. She was a formidable woman who suffered – or rather those downwind of her suffered – from BO of an unbelievable pungency. When Jean asked if she could use the bath for the twins, it therefore came as no surprise to be told firmly that the bath was where the coals were kept but that she might just stretch a point this once. With equal firmness Jean informed her that she might just have to stretch several points as the twins were accustomed to a nightly bath. This completely floored the landlady, who had clearly never heard of such a thing. But she made a monumental concession by allowing Jean the use of her daughter's baby bath, though on one condition – it must be available once a month when her daughter took her baby to the children's clinic.

Another frightening aspect of this woman was that she cooked for us. Now at that time there was a glut of Glaswegian eggs. You could buy them so cheaply it wasn't worth the hens going through the strain of laying 'em. Consequently we got eggs for breakfast, dinner, tea and – when we returned from the theatre – supper. At breakfast they would be fried, at tea boiled, for lunch poached – with beans. At first she would be quite blatant about it: a quartet of fried eggs would surround the tomatoes; boiled eggs would appear in groups of three; poached eggs would come on as a duet with a backcloth of baked beans or a lavish Italian montage of spaghetti. Later – as if even she were ashamed of her egg-bound menu – she would take to burying them under piles of the ubiquitous beans or spaghetti. You could say that her meals were the henbane of our lives.

Oh, God – the sight of that shapeless woman with her wrinkled lisle stockings which, thick as they were, couldn't mask the tide-marks round her ankles! No wonder Hildegarde deserted us and returned to London.

The following year, 1957, in Edinburgh, we picked an ice-box in Howe Street – quite a fashionable district. The digs were on the first floor, reached by stone stairs. In fact the entire structure was of stone – walls, floors, the lot. We were frozen to death, the only things alive and kicking being the mice. Much to the twins' amusement a couple of the wee timorous beasties jumped out of the carpet sweeper the moment Jean started operating it. Needless to say, Jean was on the nearest chair in a trice. Not so the twins, who shouted 'More, more!'

We related this story to a reporter on the *Scottish Daily Express* and almost immediately, out of the blue, came a letter from a Mrs Lila Wildridge, inviting us to her 'warm' house. It turned out that Biddy, one of her daughters, had written me a fan letter to which, as a matter of courtesy, I'd replied. This had impressed Lila not a little, so that when she read of our plight she reacted instantly. We accepted her invitation, of course, and soon found ourselves in a home of great warmth; I as the only male was particularly spoilt! Besides Lila, recently widowed, there were my fan Biddy, her three sisters Claire, Mary and Ella, and a pillar of Scottish society in the person of the delightful nanny, Miss Dunlop. Over forty years later we are still friends. We have visited them in Edinburgh and they have been to stay with us. Ella even went so far as to hire me to act as Eamonn Andrews in *Lila Wildridge – This Is Your Life*, a celebration of her eightieth birthday in Killiecrankie in 1991.

Another of our acquaintances was ex-Chief Constable Willie Merrilees of Edinburgh, who shared with the Wildridges the role of brightest sparks in our off-stage life in that city during the late fifties. We shall never forget a party thrown for the whole company at his house by Willie and his CID colleagues. We were all handsomely wined and dined and then – lamb pies and neeps (mashed turnips) in one hand and a dirty great tumbler of Scotch in the other – were royally entertained by a trio consisting of Willie and two of his colleagues. These three, burly great blokes as they were, totally belied their appearances and proved to possess the most lovely voices. They sang 'McGregor's Lament', 'The Rowan Tree' and several other Scottish folk songs, and the singers in our company responded with those of the English variety. Tom Walling – he of the sweet tenor voice; Howarth Nuttall – manly baritone, and Pat Lambert – lovely girl with voice to match – all gave of their best, and I weighed in with 'We've been together nah for forty years' which I passed off as a Cockney ballad. Kath West contributed a few high kicks, and Bob was your Uncle!

It would be unfair to leave Scotland without mentioning another landlady who shed her ray of light on us grateful thespians. Mrs Garrow of 74 Rosemount Place made us very comfortable when we 'digged' with her in Aberdeen. What a difference it made when there were warmth and a welcome waiting after the show!

And theatrical digs of the better kind were not confined to

Caledonia. The Mansers in Eastbourne, for instance, welcomed us right royally into their home, as did the Hamilton-Fishers in Torquay. It was while staying with the latter that I constructed a dolls' house for the twins – a massive structure which our grandchildren still play with. When we left the digs it took up the entire back seat of the car, so that Jean and the girls had to return home by train!

Once, during the early days of touring in 1955, we had to undergo the third degree by a Scarborough landlady before she would let her lovely flat to us. Margaret Jowsey was the lady and her highly desirable property in Scalby Road became our home for two successive seasons. She insisted on interviewing me before she would agree to let a *variety performer* cross the threshold – let alone his family.

It cost all of £5 to go to Scarborough and back by rail from London, which we thought a bit steep. Luckily she accepted me, being impressed by my clean-cut, honest face, though I have a feeling that it was my photograph of the twins that tipped the balance. Her understandable caution had a happy outcome, as we became great friends with her and kept in touch until she died twenty years later.

All these places, some highly salubrious, others rather less so, quickly became home when we were all together. Nevertheless as the children approached school age it was obvious that our gypsy existence would have to end. It was at this juncture, just on cue, that I received an offer which would keep me employed in London and make it possible for us to settle down as a family in Twickenham.

It's Friday, It's Five to Five...

It was during the winter season of 1959 that I had one of these pieces of luck that all careers need from time to time. George Inns, producer of *The Black and White Minstrel Show*, and Johnny Downes, producer of the popular children's variety show *Crackerjack*, popped in to see the show with their talent-spotting hats on. George booked me for a summer series called *Hi Summer* to go out on TV in 1960 and Johnny booked me for *Crackerjack* to start straight afterwards in the autumn.

So it was farewell to those free-wheeling Fol days and hail to the more demanding life of television. Hi Summer starred Kenneth Connor, a hero of mine. I would stand staring at him in rehearsals – when I wasn't laughing, of course – and pinch myself to prove that all this was real. Reality intervened on my first take when I collapsed with nerves and hammed it up so badly that it's a wonder I wasn't sacked on the spot. But I wasn't, and managed to redeem myself somewhat by writing a sketch called 'Listen with Father' (a skit on the much-loved *Listen with Mother*) in which I, as an Uncle Mac character, read a highly suggestive story about 'Nellie the Naughty Newt' while becoming progressively pissed. This found favour with the studio audience – so much so that it was included later in the stage version of *The Black and White Minstrel Show* at the Victoria Palace.

In *Crackerjack* I was booked as the comic and was going to need a straight man. So Johnny Downes and I took ourselves off to see Peter Glaze, who at the time was performing as understudy for one of the Crazy Gang at the Victoria Palace. I immediately saw the possibility of a double act with him, and after the show we met and agreed to give it a try.

Early in September we duly turned up for rehearsal at the studios in Ladbroke Grove. 'We' consisted of myself, Peter Glaze, Pip Hinton (a singer and comedienne, and another new recruit) and a script – not a very funny one, I'm afraid, by which I mean that I didn't think it would get much reaction from the studio audience. I was right. The lack of reaction from the three hundred children there left us all feeling particularly eggy, facewise, in front of the camera, and not for the first or last time I took refuge in nostalgia for the carefree Fol-de-Rol days.

But as every trouper must, I picked myself up and decided that next time, rather than going into battle half-armed, we'd return with guns blazin', even if it meant rewriting the script – which I often did, with much better results. From then on *Crackerjack* steadily improved.

'*It's Friday – it's five to five and it's CRACKERJACK!*' was how the show started, and for twenty-two weeks a year it went out live, from the Shepherds Bush Empire. Among other things it featured cross-talk patter between myself and Peter Glaze as well as games of a crazy nature with contestants from the audience, which would act as eliminators for *Double or Drop*, a quiz in which you had to answer a series of questions on general knowledge posed by Eamonn Andrews, the show's compère.

If you answered a question correctly you were given a prize: if you got it wrong you received a cabbage – all of which you had to hold in your arms. The winner was the one who survived and ended up holding the most prizes and the least number of cabbages. If you dropped more than three cabbages you were given 'Out' by Gillian Comber, the fourth member of the gang – who as I've mentioned, had been an Ovaltiney and in panto with me.

The finale, which I always compiled and wrote, would be an adaptation of the pop hits of the day – in fact parodies of the most tortuous kind, one of the most outrageous being a version of 'Michelle' based on the Tour de France (the words 'Michelle, ma belle' would be accompanied by a ding-ding on a bicycle bell!). Prior to this Pip would have delivered an opening song and she, Gillian, Peter and I would have done a comedy sketch. Guest artists included Lulu; Tom Jones; Dave Dee, Dozy, Beaky, Mick and Titch; Cliff Richard; Val Doonican and top groups of the day. In those days there was no *Top of the Pops*, so one of the only outlets for pop singers was an appearance on *Crackerjack* – we were able to pick the cream of the new groups. I say 'we' but I really mean Johnny Downes and, after he left, Peter Whitmore who succeeded him as producer.

Of the guests who appeared we had trouble only with Tom Jones, a performer whose proud boast was that he wore his trousers out from the inside while gyrating his hips in a most sexy manner. This obviously satisfied the mums but left their younger children totally mystified (they were more innocent in those days!). Anyway, when he was invited back he solemnly swore that not a hip gyration would mar his performance, since he would anyway be singing that old Scottish folk song 'Speed Bonny Boat'. It didn't quite work out like that, however. He started and, lulled into a false sense of security, the camera pulled back to reveal him in his full-frontal glory – whereupon he started to produce such pelvic thrusts and hip gyrations that they immediately cut to a puzzling shot of his left ear. Poor Tom: we've had a laugh over it every time we've met since then.

A variety show at that time of day was something new, and, strangely, its appeal was not confined to the youthful audience at which it was primarily aimed. It was, for instance, the only show which publicans could watch before opening shop! To have fans in this sector of the community was a bonus which Peter and I exploited to the full, and I'm afraid we both sponged on the pub fraternity to an unconscionable degree.

We got on well socially, but working with him was more difficult. Peter Glaze's inability to learn a script, especially the 'double spot' between him and me which kicked off the show, made life very hard for both of us. He had all the leads and I had all the funny answers, so it was important for him to get it right. If only it had been possible for autocues to be around in those early days of television, his problems would have been solved. But as it was it used to make me hot and cold never knowing whether he'd get it right. I never said anything, just bottled up my anger, while feeling cold and resentful.

It has always been easier for me to keep the peace. I've hated rows, ever since I heard them incessantly at home between my parents. I vowed that I would never row with Jean or the family ever. The result has been, of course, very damaging. I have often denied myself a true expression of my feelings and this has carried on in my working life. I have always been 'nice to work with', 'he never quibbles, he just gets on with it'. Any disagreements over scripts or with fellow actors' behaviour on stage has been kept inside me and festered away. The result all too often has led to me drowning my sorrows in drink.

Anyway, after *Hi Summer*, George Inns invited me to join *The Black and White Minstrel Show*, which had started on TV in 1958. This was an all-singing, all-dancing show featuring black-faced minstrels and the leggy female TV Toppers in white-face. George Mitchell, the choirmaster, would sketch out a medley of songs to illustrate a theme. For a Day at the Races, for instance, the show would gallop into a breathless sequence of numbers from 'De Camptown Ladies Sing Dis Song' to 'Blaydon Races', with the TV Toppers performing their high kicks while the Mitchell Minstrels backed their three lead singers – Tony Mercer with his Bing Crosby bass, John Boulter, the lyric tenor, and the dramatic baritone of Dai Francis.

As the shows were live there had to be some diversionary entertainment to allow the Toppers and Minstrels to change costumes, and these would often be of a comedy musical kind. I made my début on the show during Christmas week 1960, joining Stan Stennett, George Chisholm and Val Brooks. I stayed with that series until May 1961 – still doing *Crackerjack* on Fridays. The schedule was hectic: 9.30 a.m. to 12.30 rehearsing for *Crackerjack*; then 2.30 to 5 p.m., in a different venue, rehearsing for *The Black and White Minstrels*; in any spare time I had I learned lines and wrote scripts.

In 1961, after the TV shows had stopped for the summer, we took a stage version of *The Black and White Minstrel Show* to Scarborough, playing to packed houses at the Futurist Theatre all summer. While we were there, Johnny Downes rang to tell me in confidence that *Crackerjack* was to be honoured by a visit from the Queen in the autumn. We were all delighted to hear that she wanted to visit us – afterwards we found out why. We were introduced to her by Eamonn Andrews and she spoke to us all. When it was my turn to be introduced she told me that she always watched the programme with Prince Charles and

108

Princess Anne. I was so flabbergasted that I burst out loudly: 'You don't!'

'Yes, we do,' the Queen replied, and when we both realised my breach of royal formality we laughed like mad!

Incidentally, both Prince Charles and Princess Anne came to see *The Black and White Minstrel Show* and were brought round to my dressing room afterwards. Prince Charles asked if he might have the script of 'Listen with Father' to perform at Gordonstoun, and of course I agreed. I wish I'd seen it!

The Black and White Minstrel Show opened at the Victoria Palace in May 1962, and as soon as I had finished appearing in *Crackerjack* I would dive into a taxi, standing outside with engine throbbing, for the race to Victoria through the rush hour. Many times I would get out of the taxi, walk through the stage door, hear my entrance music and walk straight on to the stage. Once the traffic jam in Victoria was so bad that I leaped out of the taxi and ran to the theatre. All I could do when I eventually got on to the stage was to look at the audience and pant heavily for a minute or two until I'd got my breath back. They must have thought I was bonkers!

The same thought must have occurred to the *Crackerjack* viewers when we once did a hospital sketch. I was supposed to be in bed ill, and another actor was detailed to come in and visit me and make me feel worse. He did that all right, but not quite in the way the scriptwriter intended. At one point he was supposed to describe a wrestling match, and in his excitement demonstrate some of the holds on me. Unfortunately he got a bit over-excited and threw me out of bed. I landed head-first on the concrete studio floor, got up and didn't remember much about the end of the sketch. Peter Glaze had a theory that this affected my reason thereafter. He could have been right: you didn't have to be barmy to work with Peter – but it helped.

Some of my favourite sequences in *Crackerjack* were the short films that Peter and I made – speeding them up so that they looked like jerky old-time movies. We made one on house decorating at 225 Richmond Road and left a mess. We also borrowed the house in which the children's piano teacher lived to do a film on removals, and made another in a children's playground. The sight of two raving idiots playing about on slides and swings was enough to interest the entire neighbourhood – we filmed all day in a London park and attracted a bigger audience than the one at the TV theatre. It's a good thing it was a silent film, otherwise some of the rude comments on our performances might have been overheard.

The great moment for me was when I took over as compère of the show from Eamonn Andrews, who had decided to accept an offer from Independent Television. Eamonn had been with the show from the beginning – the first *Crackerjack* which was based on an idea by Johnny Downes, had gone out on 12 September 1955. We all clubbed together and bought Eamonn a silver tray on which we had our signatures engraved. Dear Eamonn – we missed him very much, myself particularly since I had the terrifying job of stepping into his shoes. Thank heavens it seemed to work out all right.

On top of my theatre and television commitments I was also working in radio. In 1963 *Variety Playhouse* was still flourishing with Vic Oliver as the host. Ronnie Barker and I were partners, and providing the programme with character sketches and voices. During this period we were joined by June Whitfield, a charming, very funny girl, who we at once got on with, so much so that the producer of *Variety Playhouse*, Alastair Scott-Johnston, set up a programme starring the three of us, called *Crowther's Crowd*. It might just as well have been called 'Whitfield Wits' or 'Ronnie's Rogues', such was the equality in which we were held at the time by the listening public. Whatever our respective skills, however, we were totally unable to cope with the banality of the script. Consequently *Crowther's Crowd* was not the success it should have been. The only successful thing about it was that it brought together three people, and their spouses, who got on well. Jean and I, Ronnie and Joy (of man's desiring, as Ronnie has it), June and Tim, indulged in 'mad-cap' adventures together. Never more so than when we all played bar billiards in Littlehampton. June proved to be the most terrible loser and let forth such loud and foul oaths, she emptied the salon!

I kept up this crazy life until 1965, and to cap it all recorded *Minstrel* TV shows on Sundays.

Small wonder with the amount of work I'd taken on during the early sixties that I began to turn to booze to carry me through. One thing, however, prevented it taking a firmer hold than it eventually did – my professionalism. With rare exceptions, such as the brief twice-nightly Victoria Palace appearances, I would never drink when working – I wouldn't dare in case I forgot my lines.

Mind you, frequent games of cricket in the summer with the *Black and White Minstrels* team presented no problems, as it didn't really matter if you were slightly the worse for drink – in fact sometimes I pulled off my most spectacular catches when under the influence. One in particular springs to mind, probably because it was at the Oval and involved the South African Test player Pom Pom Fellowes-Smith. I caught him out at deep square leg – something I'd never have achieved sober.

I left the Victoria Palace in September 1965 after I'd clocked up 1,144 twice-nightly performances; during that time I had also appeared in five *Crackerjack* series and four series of the telly version of the *Minstrels*. I carried on doing *Crackerjack* for another three years but all good things come to an end – or should do. After eight years or so I felt I was getting type-cast as a children's entertainer. The cabaret bookings had tailed off and I had been offered a farce with Brian Rix, so I knew it was time to make a clean break. Tom Sloan, then head of Light Entertainment at the BBC, was furious when I told him of my decision and did his level best to talk me out of it. 'Do you know how much So-and-So is making doing children's television in America?' he said. I pointed out that the TV audience over here wasn't anything like it was in the States, and that anyway my mind was made up. He eventually relented and let me off the hook.

So in 1968 after I had joined Brian it was farewell to *Crackerjack* – and almost goodbye to my driving licence. The cast and I said farewell and I went off to the Garrick to appear in *Let Sleeping Wives Lie*. It didn't hit me until after the play that another chapter in my life had closed, whereupon I went to drown my sorrows at the Italian restaurant across the road. I climbed into my car to drive home to Twickenham and raced a car over Chiswick Bridge – it turned out to be a police car! I was stopped, breathalysed, found to be just over the limit and escorted to Richmond police station. Fortunately I was known there, having done them several good turns in the form of free cabaret for their charity nights. They filled me up with black coffee and then did another test – this time I was OK. 'You're a very lucky bastard,' the station sergeant glowered at me before allowing me to drive the one and a half miles home.

Full of remorse, I promised myself and Jean never to drink again – a promise I inevitably broke the following day. By this time Jean was becoming more and more concerned about my drinking. Because of my vow never to have family rows (a vow which incidentally I had never shared with Jean), our communication and honesty with each other was beginning to break down. Whenever she told me how worried she felt I would deny emphatically that there was any problem, saying, 'I can handle it – and anyway lots of people I know drink far more than me.' When I felt anger rising at the challenge I would make some excuse to go out – or retire and write a script. The evidence of my growing alcoholism still wasn't sinking in. I persuaded myself that I needed this constant refuelling to face the pressures I was under at the time. Indeed these pressures had been pretty fierce, dashing from one show to another, often changing *en route* in the taxi. But of course it wasn't really so, Put simply I was, like Father, an alcoholic.

Let Sleeping Wives Lie, by Harold Brooke and Kay Bannerman, opened at the Garrick Theatre in the spring of 1967 with a cast headed by Brian Rix and myself, and including Derek Farr, Elspet Gray, Anna Dawson, Leo Franklyn, Bill Treacher, Andrew Sachs and Carmel Cryan. The plot had all the ingredients needed for a good farce – an American company wanting to vet their employees' wives invites them all for a weekend in a Brighton hotel called the Hotel Bedford which, by a magical and accidental short-circuit of the electrics, became Hot Bed – new readers begin here!

The show ran for two years and during its run I remember another significant event concerning alcohol. I appeared on a programme for the BBC in a series called *Does the Team Think?* which was recorded at lunchtime. After the recording Ted Ray, Cyril Fletcher, Jimmy Edwards, and I repaired to the Captain's Cabin and got pissed – all of us. They didn't have to work at the Garrick Theatre that night, but I did. I slept in the dressing room all afternoon and did the first act that night on automatic pilot, knowing that my speech was slurred. Elspet Gray, playing my wife, asked me if I was pissed, and I denied it. After that I never had a drink before or during work. I became a binge drinker, saving all my drinking for periods when I was not required to perform as a professional – which I prided myself on being. Whenever a newspaper reporter has asked me what my pet hate is, my answer has always been unprofessionalism.

Despite this small lapse, I was, in fact never happier than working with Brian Rix. He was the last of the actor-managers, that vanished breed who believed so strongly in their craft that they were prepared to put their money where their mouths were – incidentally creating jobs for both fellow actors and production staff.

He did it all with such good humour. I put this down to his being a fellow cricket nut – though not to the extent of Frank Benson, a Shakespearian actor-manager who once put the following advert in *The Stage*: 'Wanted: actor to play Laertes. Must have a fine leg and be good at 3rd slip.' Frank's company not only excelled in the Shakespearian repertoire but could play Hamlet with an opposing team.

Apart from Brian and me, the only other cricket buff was Leo Franklyn. So there wasn't all that much interest among the cast in following the fortunes of the MCC in the West Indian Test series of 1967 during the West End run of the play. At the critical stage of the last match, when the English batsmen were slowly accumulating the runs which were to win us the game and the series, the three of us had to unglue our ears from the muted trannies in the dressing room to appear on stage. An inspired bit of casting resulted in our dresser, a delicate lad who considered cricket to be a naff game, being stood in the wings armed with a piece of chalk and a cardboard 'scoreboard' to indicate the course of the game should we choose to look offstage. We frequently so chose, and the sight of three of the most energetic actors in the piece staring into the wings and shouting 'Good show!' at intervals in the complicated plot must have put a severe strain on the audience.

Brian and his wife Elspet have remained friends over the

years, a friendship we shall always treasure. We've even been on cricketing holidays together – one never-to-be-forgotten trip in 1976 to the West Indies and another to Corfu.

It was in Corfu that the chef, one Stavros, served up something called *osso buco*, a somewhat unappetising dish which was instantly translated as 'Denis Compton's Kneecaps'. Things did improve after that, though not by much since Stavros took to appearing from the kitchen brandishing his knife like a machete and enquiring whether D.C.'s kneecaps had made a reappearance. Corfiat's idea of sarcasm. But we all got on well together and not even the menu could get us down. It was a cross between an Outward Bound course and one of the Whitehall farces.

There was one other cricketing experience that Brian and I underwent in 1968, during the run of *Sleeping Wives*. This was a debacle of a game in Hull – Lord's Taverners XI *v.* Hessle CC, Hessle being a suburb of Hull and the occasion a celebration of one hundred years of cricket on the ground. Brian, as a Hullite, was invited by the Taverners to be match manager, a responsibility which he undertook with uncharacteristic seriousness, bringing all his stage managerial skills to the formation of his team. He even included Taverners who were natives of Hull or thereabouts: John Alderton, Pauline Collins, Ian Carmichael and Alan Plater, plus a sprinkling of likely lads who were there to get us out of trouble – John Edrich and John Snow, to name but two.

As his co-star, I was honoured to be asked to open the batting with him, but hadn't bargained for what followed – though I should have, knowing that he has always liked nothing better than succeeding. He suggested that a spell in the nets at Alf Glover's Cricket School was necessary to fit us for the fray, a proposal which I'm afraid I treated with the levity I thought it demanded. 'It's a charity match, Brian love. So long as we turn up and wave a bat. . . .'

Too late I realised that I'd said THE WRONG THING. Turning upon me a gaze of deep sincerity, he replied: 'I'm a Yorkshireman and there's one thing I hold more sacred than Geoffrey Boycott's birthday and oratorio – and that's cricket.'

When the day dawned I was collected by a keyed-up Brian and

we set course in his MG for Yorkshire. Turning off the Al, we passed rapidly through Goole – unkindly reminding ourselves that the town had a suicide pact with Grimsby – and arrived at the Hessle ground to be greeted by a large and expectant crowd. Brian won the toss and not only elected to bat but decided that we two should open the innings, so out we went to the plaudits of the multitude. He, as the occasion demanded, took the first ball and – oh horror, horror! – was clean bowled by the first delivery.

Astonished, he kept his ground until the umpire raised an index finger heavenwards. Only then did he stalk back to the pavilion, red of face, thunderous of brow at the injustice of it. For it was the convention in charity matches all over the kingdom that in circumstances such as this the umpire would yell out 'No ball', and give the luckless batsman another bite at the cherry.

But not in Yorkshire! When you're out there, you're on your bike. Brian's mortification was not eased when it became known that the bowler wasn't even a decent quickie from the clubs but a wing three-quarter for Hull Kingston Rovers. It was also divulged that as Brian had passed him on the way back to the pavilion he'd muttered to the umpire: 'Well, I didn't know the prat couldn't bat!'

One more anecdote before leaving Brian and Elspet, dating from a time when I was appearing with Brian in a farce on TV in which I was playing a vicar. Elspet had been admitted to hospital suffering from what is generally referred to as a 'women's' complaint', which necessitated an operation, and I thought it might be droll if I were to visit her in my vicar's garb and administer a measure of clerical cheer. I persuaded the producer, Wallace Douglas, that this was a good idea, and duly departed for the hospital where I insinuated myself into her room. And my God, it worked! Elspet was in such fits she nearly burst her stitches and had to ask me to leave the room.

Fully satisfied that my ruse had been successful, I climbed into the Daimler-Jaguar which in those days I was driving and headed for the Garrick Theatre. Halfway down the Cromwell Road the traffic lights turned red and I pulled up on the nearside. On my offside was a crowd of bovver boys packed into a Transit van. Incensed by the sight of a man of the cloth in a posh car, they began to vent their spleen by shouting such choice offerings as: 'You're a fucking lucky bastard, ain't ya – ya must've nicked the collection.'

I let them carry on in this vein until they'd exhausted their vocabulary, and in the pause between that and the lights changing I opened the window and shouted in my gruffest voice: 'Fuck orf!' The shock-horror on their faces and their narrow avoidance of a traffic bollard caused me great satisfaction.

Fourays

Appearing on television, especially in the sixties, changed my life drastically. For one thing the fan mail started cascading in. I particularly remember receiving letters from a lady calling herself 'Constant Viewer', who asked if I liked the place where she'd put my photograph – she fondly imagined that I could look out into her living room through the small screen!

Naturally I started by replying to them all. Then Jean coped with it for a while but it eventually got too much for her, at which point Joyce Brewer came into our lives and stayed to cope with my mail for twenty-five years until 1993. It was marvellous even after we'd moved to Bath. I'd just scribble something on the letters, send them on to her and she'd return lovely replies ready for me to sign and post.

Recognition is the other flattering problem, because if people like you they want to get in touch by talking to you, even accosting you in the street or in shops. Indeed, I have always gone out of my way to ensure that they do! For myself this has never been a problem, but when the children were younger it was a strain, particularly when we were on holiday or out together. During my *Crackerjack* period and for some time afterwards it got really bad. Time after time we were driven from the Science Museum or the London Zoo by young fans of mine. I had become a sort of Pied Piper figure – which was all right by me, but not for my children – and I wasn't going to let it deprive me of their company. So we started looking for a holiday home.

Soon after the start of *The Black and White Minstrel Show* at the Victoria Palace in 1962 we shared a holiday house with

117

George and Etta Chisholm and their children at Middleton-on-Sea on the Sussex coast near Bognor Regis. Jean was expecting again, and on 29 November our fourth daughter arrived.

Charlotte Louise is a drama queen – she could hardly help being so, with me as her father. She wasn't born in a trunk, as the old theatrical convention has it, but at University College Hospital in London, with me sitting by Jean learning a *Crackerjack* script. Charley has since realised her flair for acting by running her own cabaret company and works for a local professional company directing community productions, and very good they are, too. I've always held that true amateurs are pros who don't get paid, and those are the sort whom Charley works with.

It didn't take us long to find Fourays or, once discovered, to negotiate its purchase. This was early in 1965 and capital gains tax on the sale of second homes was being introduced on 1 April, so the Renshaws, who owned it, were anxious to sell. They were very nice people and proved over-generous in the amount of furniture, fixtures and fittings they left for us. I think they felt that a family was moving in which would love and respect Fourays as much as they had done.

The acquisition of a second home caused untold ribaldry in the ranks of the *Minstrels* – 'Crowther's Towers' was among the more printable names bandied about. We actually thought of calling it *Seven Seas*, but Nicholas was on the way by then, and with the complications of that particular pregnancy we thought that anything with a seven in it would be tempting providence!

We moved in at Easter 1965, before Nicholas was born, and embarked on the first of what were to be many 1930s-type holidays. On the appointed day we all climbed into the cars and set off for the Sussex coast. Besides the six of us there were Monserrat, our Catalonian au-pair, and Pyramus, our highly intelligent poodle – Pirrie for short. Thisbe, our Russian blue cat, stayed in London. As we passed the Sussex county sign we all cheered mightily (we still carry on this tradition when we pass the Avon county sign). Passing through Pulborough, Pirrie started to whine and fidget – I think he could smell the ozone by then.

Finally we arrived. Pirrie leaped out, barking with joy, and started to chase seagulls, while the children climbed on to their bikes and were not seen for some time. Jean, Montsy and I entered the house and immediately felt as if we had been welcomed by an old friend. The family were to stay for the whole of the school holidays. I returned to London to work, but would get down at weekends and for a couple of nights after the show.

Eight weeks after moving in, on 10 June 1965, Nicholas James arrived – the last and luckiest. He was a rhesus baby and had to have his entire blood supply changed at birth by transfusion. At one point after he and Jean had returned home he became so anaemic that we had to drive back to the hospital to get him topped up. I don't know who the donor was, but he must have been related to Sherpa Tensing as Nicholas was an ace climber, abseiling the nursery cot with ease.

It was all quite a trial, but Jean and I wouldn't have had 'em any different. The children have certainly introduced us to some fascinating characters: to Mary Lee, for instance, the sister in charge of the post-natal ward at UCH where Charly and Nick were born. Mary was Irish, and possessed that special kind of feminine logic to which there is no answer. She once sounded off to a London policeman who had stopped me, quite correctly, for driving the wrong way down a one-way street, as directed by herself. 'Nonsense, man – I walk up here every day.' Gobsmacked, he retired beaten.

Armed with this precious gift and a fervent Christianity, Mary Lee faced life and all it could throw at her with energy and courage. Her base was a Bloomsbury mews flat which was a haven for anyone requiring help, its modest accommodation seeming to expand and contract accordingly. Occasionally she would leave Base and home in on her Target for Tonight – which frequently included Jean. This was especially welcome around Christmastime, when Jean would be glad of a helping hand. Surrounded by a growing family and a workaholic husband she needed all the help she could get. It was a sad day when God decided that he wanted Mary for himself: she died of cancer on 15 January 1991.

Oh, the dream-like times we spent at Fourays, with strange,

dream-like people! The Hardings, for example – she the cleaner, her husband the gardener. He had a petunia fixation. No sooner would Jean have got rid of them during one visit than they would reappear on the next. 'Lovely bit of colour,' he would say. Mr H also took to patrolling outside the kitchen window whenever we had company, doffing his cap and shouting 'Good morning!' as he attempted to identify such of our theatre friends as might be inside. If he failed on the first attempt he would make another circuit and repeat the cap-doffing and greeting. Sylvia Syms, June Whitfield, Ronnie Barker and many more were chalked up in this way.

Sylvia, then at the peak of her career as a film actress, worked with us in a charity called SOS (the Stars' Organisation for Spastics); she was later to play my wife in the TV series *My Good Woman*. June Whitfield and Ronnie Barker both performed with me, of course, on radio's *Variety Playhouse*, and then in the radio series *Crowther's Crowd*.

Our next door neighbours were Nigel Patrick – at that time very big in films – and his wife, Beatrice Campbell. I don't think 'Paddy' relished the idea of a 'variety pro' next door, but once it occurred to him that I might be a relatively intelligent fellow and one who was not in the habit of exclaiming 'I say, I say!' every time I spotted him pruning his roses he mellowed, and Bea and he proved delightful hosts. They would invite us in for lethal cocktails – so lethal that on one occasion Jean had to ask Merle, yet another au-pair, to cook lunch.

Down at Fourays there were magical tracking competitions using pebbles to form arrows. It didn't really matter if you got lost because the trail always ended up at the fish and chip shop, whose products would be consumed on the way back home. Then there were the treasure hunts and quizzes. The children would be given the clues in the form of tortuous rhymes and off they would rush on their bicycles to solve them, leaving us to sunbathe in peace. This was all right in principle but difficult in practice, especially if it involved members of the general public, which one clue certainly did:

With Ronnie Barker and
June Whitfield during the
radio recording of
Crowther's Crowd.

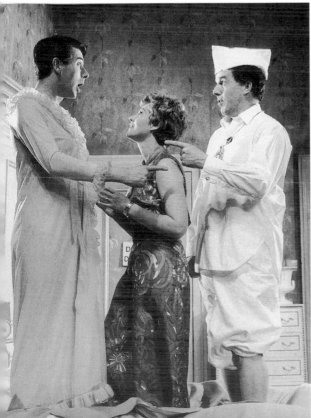

With Brian Rix and Rona
Anderson in *Let Sleeping
Wives Lie*, 1967.

Top of the Bill: Wellington Pier: Great Yarmouth, 1970.

Four men with but a single thought: Harry Worth, Peter Noone, Leslie
Crowther, Sid James. (below) With the 'Y Fronts'.

With Sylvia Syms in *My Good Woman*.

Eamonn Andrews throws a googlie with his little red book. . .

Charity rounds. . .

ith Bud Flanagan during the run of *Underneath the Arches*.

op of the ratings again with *The Price is Right*.

With Jean at home.

Stars in Their Eyes.

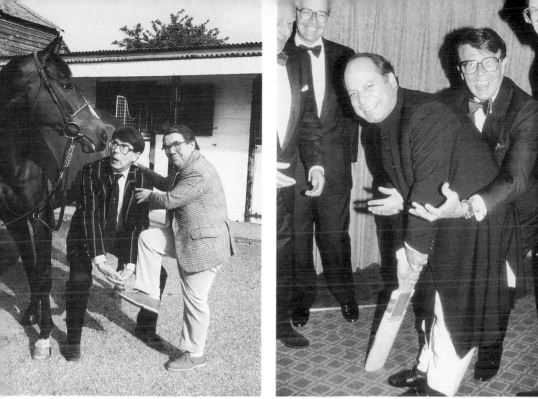

(top left) At Goodwood with Ronnie Corbett for Lord's Taverners. (top right) Brian Johnston, John Major and the Prime Minister of Pakistan.
(bottom right) An early morning visit from Patrick Shervington on Lord's Taverners' business. . .
(bottom left) Holding court at the Taverners.

Leaving hospital. . .

A holiday with Jean at Gleneagles.

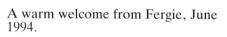

A warm welcome from Fergie, June 1994.

> From London I travel
> I don't have to drive
> What time does the last one
> At Bognor arrive?

One by one they would race to the station to obtain the answer. Ginny Patrick, Nigel and Bea's daughter, got shouted at by the stationmaster: "'Ere, what's this? You're the umpteenth kid who's asked me when the last London train arrives. Clear off!'

Mind you, had he known that they were connected with Mrs Jean Crowther he wouldn't have been surprised. Mary Lee came often for weekends and Jean would turn up at Bognor Station to pick her up only to be greeted by a message over the public address system: 'Will Mrs Jean Crowther kindly go to Chichester Station to pick up Sister Mary Lee.' Poor darling Mary – once again she'd got on the wrong end of the train, which separated at Barnham.

Mary spent many New Years with us at Fourays during the 1960s. Christmas itself was always celebrated at home in Twickenham. Our mahogany dining table, which had been Jean's Granny's, was large and oblong and did yeoman service for both the Stone family and the Crowthers. A truly Dickensian festival it would be.

One marvellous tradition which we kept up for a while was a show put on by the children in the attic playroom on Christmas afternoon. No modesty about them – it was always called *The Star Show* and we grown-ups would usually end up crying with laughter.

For several Christmases during the sixties I'd be getting up at the crack of sparrow-fart in order to see the joy on our children's faces as they unwrapped their presents and we were unwrapping ours – this before the BBC car came to take me to Queen Mary's Hospital for Sick Children at Carshalton, where we regularly did live shows on Christmas morning. Oh, the joy of doing those shows – of having the chance to do them, having left our brood of healthy children at home. Only once was I floored, and that was when I received a present from a young boy, on camera. The trick was that I would chat up a

121

child on camera and then magically produce a toy, specially chosen, which I would present on behalf of the BBC.

I was interviewing a very sick little boy and had just got out the words: 'Well, we've got a present for you, young man', when he came back quick as a flash with 'And I've got one for you, too' and produced it, gift-wrapped. It was a total surprise and one that struck at my heart, so much so that I had to kick my ankle hard in order to suppress the tears which came unbidden to my eyes. It worked, too – when I later looked at my ankle it was quite swollen and bruised.

On Boxing Day off we would charge to UCH, where the post-natal ward would be decorated with holly and ribbons. There Mary would have gathered many of the mums and dads who had passed through her care – with their offspring, of course – to have Boxing Day lunch, with the Christmas baby nestling in a crib at the foot of the Christmas tree.

After Christmas we would go off to Fourays for New Year. There are so many beautiful memories, but there's one of Fourays that I'll never forget. It was in 1977 and we were on the point of moving to our present house near Bath. We had decided to sell Fourays as the family were growing fast. I was in town on some mission and Jean was at Fourays getting it ready for the next owners. I phoned her, and when she answered I could tell she'd been crying. Through her tears she explained why: Fourays was ours, whilst 225 Richmond Road, Twickenham had been inherited. And for the last thirteen years that strange rectangular 1930s house with its balcony had been 'us'.

Top of the Bill

My twenties seemed to have been spent treading water, but as I started to make inroads into my thirties I found myself swimming in the deeper waters of indecision. A theatrical career is like walking a tightrope: you make the wrong choice and you fall off.

Because I was so busy and absorbed in my career I left the running of the house and family to Jean. She made all the decisions at home and was left to do all the disciplining of the children. They at times felt anger at her firmness and over the years she said she felt she was becoming the 'Wicked Witch'. I, on the other hand, always bent over backwards to be 'Mr Nice' and have fun with them whenever I had some free time. I loved them all, but still didn't realise I was putting my work first and taking my family for granted.

In the mid-sixties Leslie Grade (brother of Bernard Delfont, the impresario, and Lew Grade, head of ATV) invited me to join his organisation, London Management. I accepted, and towards the end of the decade Leslie's son Michael became my agent. One episode during this period which nearly sank me without trace was a situation comedy series on television called *Reluctant Romeo*. This was based on the unlikely premise that I was God's gift to women, with looks to match. It starred me and Amanda Barrie – who is God's gift to man. It had started as a one-off half-hour *Comedy Playhouse* which strangely had been a great success, but unfortunately the series just couldn't sustain it.

Luckily London Weekend Television, which had just started, had dreamed up a show called *The Saturday Crowd*. They asked me to be part of the star-studded company, and of course I accepted with alacrity. We did what was in effect concert party – a sort of TV Fol-de-Rols – and very successful it was, too. I think we were instrumental in collaring the potential weekend audience for the recently launched Independent Television. We went out on Saturdays at 5.45 p.m., 'we' being Lonnie Donegan, Anita Harris, Peter Gordeno, Susan Maughan, Sheila Bernette, Peter Hughes (the actor I'd giggled with at Richmond Rep) and me. It really was a great cast. We opened the show all sitting on stools singing and then went into a variety of sketches and musical numbers with 'quickies' in between.

Following the success of *The Saturday Crowd*, which ran for two years, Michael Grade booked me into a show that Bernard Delfont was putting on at the Wellington Pier in the east coast resort of Great Yarmouth. This was really my first time topping the bill in Summer Season. The show was called *Crowther's in Town* and I remember ringing Jean when I arrived in Yarmouth and excitedly inviting her to 'wait till you see the billing'! It was certainly worth waiting for – I was quite shaken when I drove into the town – and the *Yarmouth Mercury* followed suit with what one could only call a rave review of our opening performance:

'CRACKERJACK' START FOR CROWTHER SHOW
The Crowther Crowd moved into Wellington Pier Pavilion on Friday evening – and what a likeable bunch they are! The accent is on comedy, and the feeling is one of friendliness, a feeling that should spread to an awful lot of people before this season is over.

The first night of *Crowther's in Town* was pacy and polished, one of the smoothest I can remember in a long time, with Leslie Crowther linking the acts and finishing off with his own bill-topping spot. . . .

It was followed with more of the same, which modesty forbids me to regurgitate.

Topping the bill presents all kinds of problems. You're only as good as your last performance, and you're constantly in demand – more so in Summer Season because you're resident and thus trapped. I opened every fête, played in every charity football match, did every midnight matinée and rode in every donkey Derby that I could fit in round my twice-nightly stint at the theatre. I even accepted offers from the nearby resorts of Lowestoft and Gorleston. I really was a workaholic – so much so that I featured regularly on almost every page of the weekly *Yarmouth Mercury*. This gave rise to a highly perceptive comment by C. Denier-Warren, an elderly actor who was at the time appearing in a farce starring Sid James at the town's Windmill Theatre. I was later told that one day – it was during my *Crowther's Crowd* run – John Inman, with whom he was sharing a dressing room, had come in and with a great flourish flung a copy of the *Yarmouth Mercury* on the floor with the complaint: 'I'm never going to buy the rag again. There's not one photo of my dear Leslie on any page!' There was a pause, then C. D. W. said drily: 'I should hang on to it if I were you – it's probably a collector's piece!'

Workaholism! As the word implies, it's not unrelated to the other 'ism' from which I suffered, and is indeed recognised as an aspect of alcoholism. When you've got that problem, throwing yourself into your work can stop that thinking feeling! People-pleasing also comes into it and I suppose, to be fair to myself, I've always had application in anything I've set myself to do – such as the music scholarship achieved under less than ideal conditions. Tommy Trinder told me years later, when we were working together in panto, that he'd gone through just such a frantic phase the first time he'd appeared in Summer Season – to such an extent that after he'd packed up and was driving home he passed a church fête, stopped and opened it out of habit!

The Wellington Pier show was loosely based on *The Saturday Crowd* and the cast included Sheila Bernette, Peter Hughes, The New Faces and that droll ventriloquist Arthur Worsley, not forgetting his doppelgänger Charlie Brown.

We broke the box office record with our show that year – 1970 – which, considering the opposition we had in Great Yarmouth at the time, was quite an achievement. In addition to the Sid James farce at the Windmill, Herman's Hermits were at the ABC and Harry Worth was appearing at the Britannia Pier.

Dear Harry! I recall one of his lines: 'It's not when the audience stops laughing – it's when they start walking towards you!' We all got on well together, joined up for charity nights and mucked in at the football (where we ran out of yellow cards!). Sid James and I were on the same wavelength, I suppose because we were both 'actors', with aspirations towards the so-called legitimate theatre (which of course implied that mere variety artists were just a lot of bar-stewards!).

The major drawback to appearing on a pier is that there's only one way of leaving the theatre: in other words, you're trapped. The audience, having really enjoyed the show, would naturally want a chat and an autograph, so there they would be, lying in wait with programme, bus ticket or even a Kleenex tissue. Try signing one of those when all you can think of after doing two shows back-to-back is home and a kip!

The children were still at school when we opened in June but we had rented an old rectory at Burgh Castle, seven miles outside Great Yarmouth, for the school holidays. I was missing them all considerably and will never forget the morning they arrived. We'd arranged to meet off the road from Lowestoft, and I was parked in a lay-by waiting to guide the family through the lanes to the house. Suddenly round the corner came the blue Peugeot 404, luggage piled on the roof-rack, Jean at the wheel, Monserrat beside her and Pirrie the dog much in evidence. They'd been looking out for me, and when I was finally spotted there was a blast of the horn and children hanging out of every window, arms waving like mad so that the whole assemblage looked like a huge Crowtherian octopus!

Then it was on to the Old Rectory and the fun of sorting out sleeping arrangements and exploring the house and grounds. There was a tiny Saxon church next to the house with an old organ driven by bellows. Caro's eyes lit up when she saw it, and one morning I awoke to the sound of 'Cow-Cow Boogie' wafting through the air from the direction of the church – it was a tune I'd taught her and she'd roped in the others to pump the bellows for her.

Another charming occasion was when Charley and Nick came home late for lunch with their T-shirts and shorts caked in mud. Diligent enquiry wrung from them the admission that they'd helped a grave-digger dig a grave for an old lady's funeral. Not only that but, learning that the old lady (whose name, coincidentally, was Charlotte) had no other mourners, they'd stayed on for the burial. On a more constructive note the twins helped our farmer-neighbours, Ron and Jessie McLeod, to serve cream teas in their tearoom on the banks of the Yare, which ran through their farm.

That summer we had a never-ending stream of visitors – it was like running a hotel. There were also wonderful days out on the Broads and visits to Norwich, Aldeburgh and lovely Southwold. But the new school term came round all too soon and, early in September Jean and the family returned to Twickenham, while I finished the season sharing digs with Peter Hughes and Sheila Bernette.

After the strenuous summer season in Great Yarmouth, and with the prospect of a Royal Command Performance, a TV variety series, and pantomime at the London Palladium within the period of the next three months, I began to get terrible hot flushes during the day. I went to my doctor, who took my blood pressure. It was horrendously high. He told me to cut down on my smoking. He did not know about my drinking, which had been heavy all summer. I cut out smoking completely for a month and the high blood pressure disappeared. I cut down on my drinking only because I was working so hard that I literally didn't have the time.

I recorded a series of variety shows for television called *Crowther's in Town*, to which despite its title I had little or nothing to contribute apart, that is, from being a compère and introducing some of the glitziest stars in the world of showbiz. Mind you, I did have fun fooling about with some dear old comics – Chic Murray, Arthur English, Albert Burden and the like.

Following this I was booked to play Wishee Washee to Cilla Black's Aladdin in the 1970 Christmas pantomime at the London Palladium. So I was reviving my old love affair, after a fifteen-year lapse, in the kingdom's top pantomime venue, and playing the principal comic part of young brother to the principal boy – none other than scintillating Cilla! The rest of the cast included Alfred Marks as Abanazer,

Terry Scott as the Widow Twankey and Basil Brush as Basil Brush.

Cilla was fun to work with and charming to all, but I had a bit of a problem. It was customary to bring your own material to the show, but I couldn't because I hadn't got any! Realising this, my astute agent Michael Grade called in Laurie Lupino Lane, that doyen of slapstick comedy, and together we worked hard at clothing my histrionic nakedness – far harder than anyone in their right mind would work purely in the cause of comedy.

I have always been unreasonably upset by adverse criticism or bad publicity in the press, especially if deep down I thought it was justified. In the Palladium pantomime of 1970–71 I knew I had not provided enough good solid material for myself – nor indeed had I really bothered to get any. It was a time of low self-confidence for me. I used to drink to make that feeling go away, and consequently never got down to organising myself any appropriate material. Naturally I did not get good notices, and I was very angry – especially with myself.

The pantomime ran twice-daily until Easter and by the end, after what Jean called a monastic existence, we were going spare. I would leave the house at 11 a.m., do the two shows, and clock in back home at 11 p.m. Small wonder that in the theatre we relieved the strain by amusing ourselves off-stage. Alfred Marks had the dressing room next to mine and the dividing wall was anything but thick. He was given to hammering on it whenever I had visitors to ask us please to shut up as '. . . I've got some fucking nuns with me!' – all delivered in Alfred's deadpan voice. Small wonder that my guests felt rattled!

After the last performance we took ourselves off, *en famille* plus Mary Lee, to Switzerland – our version of the romantic tour with myself cast in the role of tourmaster (as you might say, a Swiss role). It was great fun and we thoroughly enjoyed it, especially as the twins were now sixteen and we thought it would probably be our last holiday together as a complete family.

On our return home Michael Grade told me that he'd received a firm offer from the Fairfield Halls at Croydon to put on a *Leslie Crowther's Christmas Party* at the end of 1971. He added that this time I must make sure I had material, and suggested a 'giveaway' number for my first spot.

I welcomed the booking. I'd finished the panto, was doing Summer Season at Paignton, and thought this would be something a bit novel. And, as ever, the assurance of work kept the lurking insecurity of the thespian at bay. It wasn't until halfway through the year that I twigged what I must do. The Big Idea came to me while I was waiting to go on in cabaret at La Taverna, Epping. I'd done the band call (the musical rehearsal with the band for my act) and afterwards had a two-and-a-half-hour wait. I spent it sitting in the band room thinking about that opening spot, and by the time I went on I'd got it all worked out. It would be the Twelve Days of Christmas but with a difference, substituting comical items for the traditional gifts: two toilet rolls, three Smith's Crisps (one burst to give the audience a refreshing shower), four Murray Mints, five Oxo cubes and so on.

I tried it out when the show opened on Christmas Eve and knew when I chucked the two toilet rolls into the audience and watched them unravel that I was on to a winner. Mind you, when they chucked them back at me I began to change my mind! That version of the Twelve Days of Christmas became my opening number for every pantomime I appeared in subsequently, and it never let me down.

Another spot which I introduced to the *L.C. Christmas Party* and followed on in several Summer Seasons and pantos was a send-up of David Bowie which I'd first done on TV in an Engelbert Humperdink show. Dressed up in a wig, platform shoes and blue satin costume, I had a backing group called The Y-fronts which included a tiny clown with a face which made the audience howl with laughter – Johnny Vyvyan. He'd been a stooge for Des O'Connor before joining me. Bless poor Johnny – we were together, winter and summer, for years. Sadly, he died in 1984.

I was to perform in several more pantos before I gave it up in 1989 for the unhappy reason you will discover. Perhaps the most rewarding was *Babes in the Wood*, played at the Theatre Royal in my home town, Nottingham, in 1973. It was a thrill to walk up Theatre Street from Old Market Square, look up and see my name in banner headlines on the front of the old Royal. On stage I could raise my eyes and wink at young Leslie, peering over the rail in the front row of the dress circle. That Christmas, too, I was joined by an old Fol-de-Rol colleague, Jack Tripp, who was playing Dame – and what a superb Dame he was!

Over the road from the stage door was the Bluebell, a pub run by Eddie and Shirley Hand, which featured prominently in my drinking days. They were a great couple and on one occasion even shut the downstairs bar so that Jack Tripp and I could celebrate. I don't know what Jack was celebrating but I certainly felt it was my birthday. What I do remember is that we both did a strip to the appropriate music!

One opening I will certainly never forget was the one at the Theatre Royal, Bath in 1979 when I was again playing Wishee Washee in *Aladdin*. One of the staff had told me that there was a legend of a butterfly connected with the theatre – and indeed I found a huge replica tortoiseshell hanging in the flies when I first stepped back-stage. I learned that tradition dictates that it must always be there during the run of a pantomime. Apparently, when Reg Maddox, manager and producer of the 1948 pantomime, was lighting the Butterfly Ballet in *Aladdin* he dropped dead of a heart attack. Ever since then, the legend goes, his ghost in the form of a tortoiseshell butterfly appears as a sign that the pantomime is going to be a success. Hence the precautionary hanging of the butterfly backcloth in the flies!

I must say that nothing was further from my mind when I prepared in the wings to make my first entrance in the Boxing Day matinée, but then a miracle happened. After Reg Maddox had allowed me sufficient time to establish rapport with the audience he fluttered down from the spotlight in the form of a tortoiseshell butterfly and alighted on my left shoulder! I gently scooped it/him up and then released it/him in the wings, meanwhile telling the audience that I would tell them at the end of the performance why I was looking so gob-smacked – which I did.

Dear old Reg – he stuck around for days and days. Sometimes we spotted him in the front of the house and sometimes back-stage, but I'll never forget the first time he fluttered down from the spotlight. And yes! The pantomime was a big success.

As the seventies gave way to the eighties I saw a change coming over the audiences – in fact they stopped behaving as pantomime audiences should. Hooligans began to appear who, when free of their handlers, would run amok. The low point came in 1989 when we were doing *Robinson Crusoe* at the Ashcroft Theatre, Croydon. David Griffin went on as Bluebeard the Pirate, villain of the piece, and was barracked by the younger element in the audience and told to get off. When Roger Kitter as the Dame made his entrance with 'Good evening, boys and girls', he too got heckled.

'We've heard it,' they shouted back.

Forewarned, I cut that line out when it was my cue but it didn't stop them from nearly ruining my 'First Day of Christmas'. All they were interested in was grabbing whatever was thrown at them.

By the end of the run I had lost all taste for pantomime and resolved that it should be my last one. In any case I was beginning to see my future very much in television terms. My first love was, and will always be, the theatre – but I couldn't ignore the fact that TV is where the money is and that, whatever success you had in a West End farce, the billing would depend on your success as a TV personality. Burning my boats, I gave the band parts of 'The First Day of Christmas' to Roger Kitter.

So ended my long affair with pantomime. I've still got panto costumes in the attic, along with other comedy props, and that's where they'll stay. But with the possible exception of Croydon I wouldn't have missed any of it for the world.

Top of the Ratings

With the small screen looming ever larger in my sights, I began to give serious thought to the kind of vehicle which might transport me to the heights to which I aspired. Dick van Dyke, an American comedian, had long been a favourite of mine. During the sixties *The Dick van Dyke Show* had been running on British television and I had watched it with envy. Here was a situation comedy where the comedian was allowed to play himself. Would that I could find something like this for myself!

I unburdened myself to Michael Grade who set up a meeting with a writer, Ronnie Taylor, and together we discussed all sorts of ideas and possibilities. In the summer of 1971 *Crowther's in Town* was playing at the Festival Theatre in Paignton with a cast which included a comedian destined soon to become a household name – Larry Grayson. It was here, while I was in Summer Season, that Ronnie Taylor brought me an outline script for what was to become *My Good Woman*.

The basic idea was that I would play an antique dealer working from home (thus making me available most of the time) with a charity-obsessed wife and a bachelor neighbour who was my friend and ally. There was a fourth character – the local vicar – who would always be seeking help to cope with his charities and parochial duties. It was a situation which I could readily identify with my own life. Jean was at that time chairman of the local committee of the Save the Children Fund as well as working twice a week in a Citizens' Advice Bureau. Many times I'd come back from rehearsals and fallen over a box of collecting tins or a bag of jumble as I walked through the door.

From these beginnings sprang the phenomenally successful three-year run of *My Good Woman* and the realisation of an ambition which most variety artists will admit to if they are honest with themselves – to be what used to be termed a 'legitimate' actor. The strange thing is that most comedians are natural actors when, as the Bard has it, 'they are put on'. I would cite Reg Varney and the late Les Dawson as supreme examples of the actor successfully emerging from the comic.

It was Michael Grade who came up with the humdinger of a suggestion that my old friend Sylvia Syms should play my wife. The other key members of the cast were Keith Barron as the neighbour and Richard Wilson as the vicar. It was Keith who, when I asked him for tips on 'proper' acting, gave me the advice which stood me in good stead then and has done many times since: always listen to what the people acting with you are saying – not forgetting to get your own lines into your head! Richard Wilson was wonderfully funny as the vicar, and many a time I had to bite my lip to stop myself laughing at his performance. After one episode when I had been teaching him to drive I had a blood blister inside my lip for several days.

The first series went out on television in February 1972 and got a very good response. We made five series in all and in the week of 8 December 1973 we were top of the ratings, beating *Coronation Street*, *Some Mothers Do 'Ave 'Em*, *The Generation Game* and even the Royal Command Performance. In fact, at the end of 1973 the show was number ten in TV's top twenty for the whole year. It's always amazed me that no repeats have ever been shown.

I really enjoyed making that series, and having Sylvia as my leading lady was a joy – though not always unconfined. I say this because of a particular incident which occurred during a warm-up session before the studio audience when dear Sylvia, game as usual, followed my recitation of a mildly naughty limerick with one which was somewhat ahead of its time, even a decade after that famous legal case which Philip Larkin celebrated in his poem '*Annus Mirabilis*':

Sexual intercourse began
In nineteen sixty-three
(Which was rather late for me) —
Between the end of the *Chatterley* ban
And the Beatles' first LP.

My offering was on the following lines:

There was a young Scotsman named Sandy
Who went into a pub for a shandy.
He whipped off his kilt
To wipe what was spilt
And the barmaid said, 'Blimey, that's handy!'

which Sylvia capped with:

A lady named Emily Post
Once had an affair with a ghost.
Said this pale ectoplasm
While approaching orgasm
'I feel that I'm coming – almost.'

A stunned silence marked that historic moment when the boundary between acceptable music hall vulgarity and pure filth was crossed, and thoughts too deep for words could almost be seen passing behind my leading lady's normally bright eyes. Of course, these days stunned silences occur only if the jokes are too mild. *O tempora; o mores*!

Since I was playing the part of an antiques dealer I wasn't surprised to receive a letter from the organisers of the first International Antiques Fair at Earls Court in January 1973, asking if I would make a celebrity appearance. I was looking forward to it, antique collecting being a hobby of mine, and had arranged to meet Jean there at 4 p.m. I was keyed up, but not as keyed up as the secretary who met me – a sophisticated, middle-aged lady who seemed excessively nervous. Jean was late (held up in traffic), and the lady indulged in several gin and frolics. I tried to calm her down, saying that I didn't mind waiting, but this seemed to get her more and more agitated.

I should have guessed that something was afoot after Jean had arrived and we set off. I should have known it when I turned down one of the corridors on a mini-tour of inspection and could see at the end of that particular corridor TV lights and cameras. I delicately enquired why they were there. 'Ah,' replied the secretary, 'it's just closed circuit – we're doing it for our own records.' She paused in front of a sedan chair. 'Look inside,' she said. I hesitated, deep in contemplation as to why the lady should want me to do this. She then delivered a shrewd come-on: 'There's a very rare pot-lid inside.' I'd been collecting Victorian pot-lids for fifteen years, and as they represented two-thirds of my antiques collection I needed no further invitation.

I duly opened the sedan chair door, only to discover Eamonn Andrews, my old mate from *Crackerjack*, clutching the dreaded Red Book and uttering the doom-laden words: 'Leslie Crowther – this is your life!' There is a photograph inside the Red Book which Thames TV presented to me later, showing me with my jaw halfway to the floor. I can remember thinking: 'Why are the Thames production team spending all this time and effort on me?'

After they'd caught me I was whisked off to the Euston Road studios of Thames and locked into a hospitality room – presumably in case I had thoughts of escaping. I remember sitting there and mulling over those people in my life whom I might conceivably fail to recognise when I heard a brief snippet of their voices before they put in the physical appearance.

But I needn't have worried: not so far as the first five guests were concerned anyway – they were my children! One contribution which was both unusual and memorable was Dickie Henderson's. From an ice-rink in Canada where he was appearing he introduced a children's choir from Ipplepen in South Devon singing 'All Things Bright and Beautiful'. This really floored me – I'd last heard them sing it the previous year when I'd introduced them at the Stars Ball for the charity SOS. They'd sung a selection of Christmas carols to Dickie, who'd taken over from me as chairman. It had floored Dickie then and he'd shed a tear: I don't think I'd ever seen Old Laconic so deeply moved. Difficult to reconcile that picture with the man who on one occasion, when stopped in an Eastbourne street, had listened patiently to a lady while she berated him unmercifully on the poor quality and lack of variety in his act. When she finally paused for breath, Dickie had delicately enquired whether she had any more goodies in her diplomatic bag.

What an evening! We had a marvellous party afterwards, all together, including my old Scottish friend William Ritchie, who'd never been further than Glasgow before – and Charlotte who was in a panic because she hadn't done her homework! But I still wondered why I'd been chosen.

Well, I suppose it was some indication of my worldly success. Undoubtedly the successful run of *My Good Woman* had put me at the top of the ratings, and I was now even more in demand for store openings and other commercial spin-offs as well as after-dinner speaking engagements.

I can't recall exactly when it was that the organisers of charitable functions in the Twickenham area came to realise my potential as a fete-opener, but it must have been about 1961 when I first appeared in *Crackerjack*. The fact that I didn't charge probably weighed heavily with them, and once their faith in my drawing powers had been vindicated there was little hope of reprieve from the charity round.

I remember following the charitable course of a tin of venison soup from a spring function of the 1st Whitton Scout Group to an autumn fete in aid of the elderly of Barnes. By then it was so battered that I took pity on it and bought it, but later lost my nerve and returned it to the charity circuit at a church fete.

Thus commenced a wonderful and continuous association with charities of every kind, whether local or national. From then on I have never been able to refuse an invitation to open a fete or make an appearance in support of one worthy cause or another. Once, when I was finding it particularly difficult to cope with the avalanche of invitations, I asked Brian Rix for his advice on what to say when approached by fete organisers. 'Your problem,' he replied, 'is that you're an easy touch, doing it for nothing. What you want to do is charge a fee and promise to pay it over to a charity of *your* choice.'

I'd just appeared in cabaret at the Normansfield Ball at the Dorchester Hotel, which Brian and his wife Elspet had organised in aid of Normansfield Hospital in Teddington, the specialist Down's syndrome centre where their daughter Shelley was living.

'Oh, yes,' I replied, 'and which charity would you recommend?' fully expecting him to say 'Normansfield'. But he didn't: SOS was his suggestion – Stars' Organisation for Spastics – the charity formed in 1954 to care for people stricken by cerebral palsy. I readily accepted his suggestion, and so began a long and happy association with SOS which continues to this day. Wilfred Pickles, Dame Vera Lynn, Maudie Edwards, David Jacobs, Brian and Elspet Rix, Dickie Henderson and Sir Harry Secombe were among those whose inspiration it had been to set up the charity and with whom I found it a joy to work.

SOS also ran Colwall Court, a holiday home for handicapped children and their parents at Bexhill-on-Sea. Here the children could enjoy a much-needed holiday while the parents took a break from the strain of constant nursing. Some years later, after I had become associated with it, SOS again lived up to its name by purchasing Wakes Hall near Colchester for the accommodation of men and women whose physical incapacities had led to their being wrongly incarcerated in homes for the mentally handicapped. Rescuing them from years of misery to give them a new life here was wonderfully worthwhile. One resident studied for and was awarded a BA (Eng) honours degree, and there have been many other successes.

In 1967, after four years with SOS, I had the great honour of being appointed chairman. The first thing I did after settling myself into the chair was to propose that we spend all the money lying idle in the funds on some worthwhile objective. This we did, building Good Neighbours' House in Camberwell in conjunction with the local authority.

What Brian – and others – perhaps failed to understand in all this was that my inability to say 'No' to approaches from charities stemmed from my people-pleasing personality, which was and is one of the more surprising manifestations of alcoholism. Certainly this taking on of all comers – in both the charitable and regular entertainment fields – has led to some fraught situations over the years, particularly when my absences happened to coincide with domestic arrangements at weekends or – more seriously – forthcoming anniversaries.

Fairly early in our marriage Jean came to realise that the only two birthdays I could be guaranteed to remember were my own and Jesus Christ's. Hers, on 12 May, and our wedding anniversary, 27 March, would often plunge me, like other husbands, into hot water or what is perhaps worse – a cool silence, maintained throughout most of the Critical Day and deepened if anything by my puzzled 'Is it anything I've done?' and the clipped rejoinder, accompanied by a shrug of the shoulder, 'No.'

Eventually Jean devised a cure for this kind of marital amnesia which was both effective and entertaining. Immediately after my birthday she would get hold of my diary and insert aide-mémoires in the following terms each week up to the Critical Day: 'It's only . . . shopping days to my wife's birthday' followed by: 'It's my wife's birthday next week. Have I bought her a present?' Much better than a sultry silence – and it almost always worked.

The absentee weekend problem would be dealt with in a similar way. On at least one weekend a month Jean would write 'YOU DARE!' across the Saturday and Sunday pages of my diary, emphasising the point that marriage is about sharing – including time. I grew to respect those weekends – and so did Michael Grade, my agent. Whenever I was offered a Sunday concert he would ring up and ask: 'Are you free or is it a You Dare weekend?'

One thing I've always felt about working for charity – it should be joyous, otherwise what's the point? Certainly I've always found it an incredibly happy experience, which I've shared with many variety stars.

Well, almost always. A notable exception which comes to mind is associated with one of those two famous showbiz personalities Lew and Leslie Grade. A call from either could mean only one thing – charity: they wanted you to work for nothing. This time it was Leslie on the phone who asked me what I was doing on a particular Saturday. 'Nothing,' I replied.

'Well, you are now,' he said, going on to explain that he was on the committee of Chelsea Football Club, which had reached the final of the Milk Cup. They would be celebrating the event with a dinner at London's Portman Hotel and – wonder of wonders – required a cabaret.

'Celebration dinner!' I exploded. 'What if they lose?'

'Win, lose or draw, makes no difference,' Leslie assured me. 'They're wonderful boys. Ask Des O'Connor – he did the same thing for me last year.'

I agreed to do it on condition that he gave me two tickets – one for Nick and one for me. So we went along to Wembley, only to see Chelsea thrashed by Sunderland. Off the pitch trooped eleven men, sullen in defeat. 'That's my audience,' I remember saying to myself.

I duly turned up at the hotel to be met by the manager in the foyer. 'Hello,' he said. 'It's not the Celebration Dinner?' My assurance that it was caused a sharp intake of breath accompanied by a heavenward rolling of the eyes. 'Good luck!' he said.

I sneaked in at the back of the dining room to listen to the speaker who was on before me, and caught him in the middle of a eulogy of the Sunderland team. 'But don't you think it's wonderful,' he was saying, 'that there is another hotel in London where tonight there is a real celebration dinner featuring another team – a team which until tonight has had little or nothing to celebrate.' With that he sat down to the sound of his bottom slapping the seat – applause was not forthcoming.

'That's my audience,' I repeated to myself before rising to die on my feet. After the stony silence I left the stage after firing a Parthian shot: 'Well, if that's how you meet defeat, I sincerely hope you never win again.' After that I went straight home, climbed into bed, and assuming the pre-natal position cried myself to sleep.

The following morning the phone rang. 'I'll answer it,' said a grim-faced Jean.

It was indeed Leslie Grade on the line, and Jean let fly with some pungent phrases, ending with the warning that should Leslie Grade ever again ask her Leslie to subject himself to such a humiliation she and he would have words.

When he could finally get a word in edgeways it was to say lamely: 'I know. Mind you, they were bastards to Des last year!'

Eric Morecambe and Ernie Wise richly deserved the award of the Golden Heart of the Variety Club of Great Britain for their charity work. In November 1981 I was asked to make a short speech at a dinner in Birmingham given in their honour when the award was to be presented, and hit upon the idea of adapting Kipling's 'If':

> If you can earn your corn when fortune flouts you
> And all the world thinks one of you's a goner.
> If you can keep your head when all about you
> Are ordering LPs of Des O'Connor:
> If you can feel unwell and still be funny
> Then face the critics when they're being harsh:
> If you can say 'At least we earnt the money'
> And then pay ten per cent to Billy Marsh
>
> If you can dream and not make dreams your master
> If you can think and not make thought your aim:
> If you can meet Bernard Manning and disaster
> And treat those two impostors just the same.
> If you can sell the BBC your talents
> And still with James Hunt make commercial gems
> And then put your careers in the balance
> By leaving Auntie for Old Father Thames
>
> If you can make a slightly aging stripling
> Write verses when with admiration gripped:
> If you can make him learn his ersatz Kipling
> Then have to have a shufti at the script:
> If you can learn to choose the scripts that matter
> Then do your bank raids with your act as known:
> If you can laugh at Jimmy Tarbuck's patter
> Whilst realising it was once your own

If you can sparkle like a dry Martini
And make th'price of admission worth the cost:
If you can bluff your way into the Sweeney
And make John Thaw look like an early frost:
If you can with your timing fill each minute
And like the game you love score priceless runs —
Yours is the earth and everything that's in it
And which is more, you'll be two men old sons!

Charity and the doing of it must give you a kick or there's no point in doing it at all, and if there's one thing I enjoy more than anything else it's the company of my fellow men and women, both the charitable and those they are helping. That is why a garden fete is always of absorbing interest to me: I positively love it and I'm sure I speak for most of my fellow artistes who give every appearance of feeling the same way as I do.

The Doldrums

In 1973 I had celebrated my fortieth birthday. *My Good Woman* was high in the ratings, I'd done a hugely successful pantomime in my home town, and I seemed to be riding on the crest of a wave. But I was still refusing to face the truth about my drinking. Then the unthinkable happened. At the end of a three-year run during which we'd done five series of six episodes Ronnie Taylor dried up – or perhaps became disenchanted. Whatever happened, he could no longer produce the scripts.

In 1975 we were spending the summer in a lovely house at Little Clacton while *Crowther's in Town* was playing at the Ocean Theatre on Clacton Pier. While we were there Ronnie sent me some scripts for a new series called *Big Boy Now* which was to star Fabia Drake, Ronnie Lewis and me. It was duly produced by ATV, who'd done *My Good Woman*, but unfortunately this one was a failure from the start – by which I mean that it was again based, like *The Reluctant Romeo*, on too unlikely a premise. Jean had read the pilot script and pointed out its weaknesses, but to no avail. Only Ronnie Corbett could have got away with being mother-dominated *and* funny for a whole series – which indeed he did later.

It was around this time that Jean wrote me a letter threatening to end our marriage because all attempts to speak to me about my drinking had resulted in frosty denials. She couldn't understand why I could control my drinking when I was working but not otherwise – and she felt resentful and devalued.

We were, I'm afraid, a typical example of a family with this problem. There is a brilliant pamphlet published for Al-Anon

143

(the group for relatives and friends of alcoholics) called *A Merry-Go-Round Named Denial*. It illustrates exactly how we were at the time. Written as a three-act play, it explains how the illness affects everyone in the cast – as the star central character gets drunk the others around him all react in their different ways. When he refuses even to discuss it, they feel confused and hurt. Sensing this he blots out his guilt and remorse by drinking again. Everyone in the family is on the roundabout – all hurting, but unable to change anything until someone has the courage to get off. Meanwhile, they all put on a face for the outside world and smile.

It was beginning to affect our social life, too. At the parties we would go to I could feel my contribution to the evening getting duller and duller as the wine took over.

Jean's letter shook me and I cut down for a while.

There followed a series of other failures, starting with a show starring Francis Matthews, Anna Dawson, Peter Gordeno and myself. There was nothing wrong with *them* – it was just me: I seemed to have lost my nerve.

In 1976 I did a series with Lena Zavaroni called *Hi Summer* which brought memories of those days in 1960 flooding back. Lena had been a child prodigy, outright winner of *Opportunity Knocks* of blessed memory, and had an amazing voice. But this was a series to which I felt I contributed nothing – I was merely watching the others having a ball.

To cheer myself up I bought a Rolls Corniche, and the first evening that I owned it I took our dear friend Michael Bates (of *It Ain't 'Alf Hot, Mum*) out for a drive. At the time Michael had cancer and was suffering dreadfully. On returning home I went to open up the garage – which wasn't as easy as you'd think, and entailed me going through the house. On the way I'd paused to have a word with Jean. Suddenly we heard whoops and cries coming from the direction of the road, where the car was standing. It was a gang of young boys who'd come along the road, spotted the Rolls and shied stones at it, shattering the windscreen.

I felt truly sickened, and remember saying to Jean that maybe the time had come for us to move. We were in any case finding the constant noise of jumbo jets on the flight path into London Airport a misery. You could say that we talked ourselves out of Twickenham that night. Of course there was an element of 'the grass is greener on the other side of the hedge' in our deliberations – particularly in my case, as the inclination to move to pastures new is a recognised aspect of the alcoholic's character. It's known as a 'geographical' – a term which embraces any attempt to avoid coming to terms with the truth. You endeavour to make a fresh start, ignoring the fact that you've taken the problem with you.

Anyway, we had the feeling that the time was right, and the more we thought about it the more convinced we were that living conditions could be a lot more pleasant than they had become in Twickenham. Looking back, how right we were!

The summer of 1976 was long and very hot. My brother-in-law John Stone had a boat and wanted to do some sea sailing, so we agreed to swap houses for two weeks. We would use John's house near Bath for a fortnight in August, giving us time to spend with Jean's parents while John and his family went to Fourays. It was during this stay that I fell in love with Bath, so much so that I became convinced that this – Jean's native heath – was the area in which we should look for a house and settle down. Strange, really: I must be one of the few comedians to fancy moving house in order to live nearer to his mother-in-law!

Having made the decision, we were in no hurry to move. Charlotte was embarking on her O-levels and Nick still had another year to do at his prep school. I visited some estate agents in Bath to tell them what sort of property we were looking for, and they promised to send us anything they thought might interest us. We looked over a few during the year, but found none that we really liked. 'We shall know when it's the right one,' we kept telling the family. A house in Lacock, the National Trust village, looked a 'possible', so after viewing it we returned to Bath to get more details from the agents – which is how, one August morning, we saw in another Bath agent's window three photographs of a property in a village some three miles from Jean's parents' home:

COUNTY OF AVON

Set within an exclusive parklike location, being elevated and overlooking outstanding panoramic countryside views and beyond to the City of Bath. A magnificent and impressive Italian/Georgian style country residence, standing within beautiful Italian-influenced, landscaped pleasure grounds.

'Wow! Where's that?' Jean asked her father. 'I've lived in this area sixty years,' he replied, 'but I've no idea where that house is.'

We obtained the brochure from the agent and were thrilled to see that it came within our price range – but not so thrilled to hear that, though they'd had it on their books for only three days, someone else had already put in an offer and was having a survey done.

We arranged to see it the following Sunday, and I can honestly say it was love at first sight. You don't often find your dream house, but this was it. While the agent took us round we both followed him in silence, and as I stood on the terrace at the top of the steps before we left I said to Jean: 'I'd sell the Rolls for this.'

Neither of us could sleep that night because we were so excited. Getting up at 3 a.m., we made a pot of tea and wrote on the back of the brochure a list of questions to ask the agent. I rang him early in the morning and told him we wanted the house and that we too would get a survey done.

Luckily for us, a near neighbour of Jean's parents was Gordon Dunn, a well-known and respected local estate agent and chartered surveyor. 'I've always wanted to have a look at that house,' he said when I asked him to negotiate the purchase. Bless his heart, he really bought the place for us – charmed the owners and drove to London with all the particulars. He advised us to offer the asking price, which we did, and happily it was accepted.

The vendors had not got a house to move into and we were in no rush, so a completion date of April Fool's Day 1978 was agreed – the least foolish thing I ever did. We put 225 Richmond Road on the market and sold it early in 1978, and we said goodbye to Fourays too – it would be too far from Bath and had really outgrown its use. The top floor of our adjoining house at Twickenham was empty so we kept that as our London base – I needed somewhere to stay after late night cabaret or before early rehearsal starts.

Early in 1978 Thames Television asked me to take over as host in their long-running success *Whose Baby*? Of course I accepted, and filled the slot for two series. It was good fun: the idea was to identify the children of well-known parents – Jeffrey Archer, Margaret Lockwood and Dick Francis were among the many celebrities I hosted. A little later that year, too, Stork margarine signed me up to present their commercials. From now on people stopped shouting '*Crackerjack*!' at me and instead accosted me with: 'I can tell the difference!'

The Stork commercials were always shot in a superstore. We used to lie in wait – technicians, camera crew and myself – in a sort of bird hide, often consisting of a pile of Andrex toilet rolls from which a few had been removed to give me a view of the butter/margarine-buying customers. The moment a couple – it was always husband and wife – had chosen butter cheerful Leslie C. would accost them and challenge them to the Stork S.B. test – husband first, crossing everything including fingers in the hope that he would choose the biscuit spread with Stork S.B. If my silent prayer were answered I would challenge the wife to say (I hoped), 'I'll buy Stork S.B. next time for him.'

It wasn't a set-up – no both biscuits spread with Stork S.B., no professional actors – it really was an honest test. The only admission is that we did have to try again and again until we got the perfect shot, which explains why I looked pretty drained on some occasions.

Only one man refused to continue being filmed after we had successfully lured him and his other half in front of the cameras. The moment he realised he might be immortalised on the small screen he confessed that his escort wasn't his wife – he was having a dirty weekend in the Black Country!

It's strange – people would say, and still do, that I lowered myself by agreeing to take part in anything so cheap as a commercial. I would say that (a) they were bloody good fun and (b) they put two of my children, Charlotte and Nick, through Marlborough College. Also, both *Whose Baby?* and the Stork commercials rescued me from the rapid downward slope to misery and despondency – the Doldrum Years had started. It seemed to me that my TV career was on the brink, with me hanging on by my fingernails. So pessimistic was I at being offered anything that I had even set myself up for a contract with Fred Rumsey, hosting an overseas cricket tour. At this critical point Jon Scoffield, the head of Light Entertainment at Central, phoned and asked me what I was doing in the next four months.

Playing it close to my chest, I said, 'Nothing', whereupon Jon came up with a great suggestion. Why not play Chesney Allen opposite Bernie Winters as Bud Flanagan in the story of their stage partnership? I accepted immediately, assuring Jon that I could get out of my current commitments. Straightaway I rang Fred Rumsey, who saw the wisdom of my decision, let me off the hook and wished me luck. Thus it was that I arrived fresh-faced and script-laden at Elstree studios, scene of my triumphs with *My Good Woman*.

I felt immediately at home with the acting, singing and dancing which the role demanded. Bernie was certainly at home with all three, particularly the acting. Dear God, he knocked me out with that. Jon Scoffield produced it immaculately and shot it with great attention to detail, so that when it came out it was a masterpiece – something that any pro would have been proud to be involved in. It saved my bacon. Not only that – it led to several appearances for Bernie and me in Royal Command variety shows. Anchored firmly on Bernie's shoulders, I strolled with him to the tunes of 'Underneath the Arches', 'Any Umberellas', 'Run-Rabbit-Run', 'Strolling', and many more of the songs which will always be associated with Bud and Ches.

We took the stage version of the show out on tour, starting at the Congress Theatre, Eastbourne, in March 1982, though it was only when we played theatrical towns such as Brighton that we really made our mark. When we were about to go on in the matinée at the King's Theatre, Southsea we learned that the real Chesney and his wife Aleta were in the audience. I don't know about Bernie, but I was somewhat gobsmacked at the thought of strutting my brief hour under the quizzical gaze of that living legend. But it was all right. After the show Aleta gripped my arm and whispered, 'You are just like my boyfriend' – which I took to be a coy reference to Ches.

During the first four months of the tour I never touched a drink: I was having one of my periodical sobriety bouts. This particular one came to a sudden end when the show was playing Scarborough and I was staying at the Royal Hotel. It happened like this. Before the start of the tour David Conville, who was running the Open Air Theatre in Regent's Park, wrote inviting me to appear as the Master of the Greensward on 15 July 1982 when the Open Air Theatre was celebrating its Golden Jubilee. The occasion was to be graced by the presence of the Queen and the Duke of Edinburgh.

I don't know who'd dreamed up this office of no profit or whether it had any historical validity – Merrie England and all that. He was a sort of Master of Ceremonies whose principal task it was to write and speak a prologue to the evening's entertainment. But the deadline had now arrived and I could delay the writing of it no longer. So I got down to it, and as I did so something prompted me to order a bottle of good claret as a restorative to my dull spirits (well, that was my justification). Whether it worked or not may be judged by the results:

Your Majesty, Your Royal Highness, Ladies, Gentles All
Most Happy Welcome to this Sylvan Scene;
Behold the Master of the Greensward I
Though why they chose me Heaven only knows!
Mayhap the reason lies in my Apprenticeship
Which I served here in Nineteen Forty Nine —
Creeping like Snail most willingly on stage
To give my Third Watchman in Much Ado.
The play was Much Ado About Nothing
And so was my performance! I recall
My father came to see his son perform,
Turned round to buy a programme, turned back
And missed me by a yard – I'd come and gone!
So many men have come and gone my liege,
The Ben Greets, Sydney Carrolls, Robert Atkins —
What men were here.
Oh Robert, with that noble voice – and hand —

Without which hand beware all imitations! They did fight
Continual battles with the elements
And with the Min. of Works – and won them all.
And now this new and splendid auditorium
Pays fitting tribute to their glorious deeds. Surely
Their ghosts return where once they loved to play.
No theatre hath Nobler Visitors. Yet today
We have a nobler visitor – Tis thee!
The first time that Your Majesty has graced
This noble theatre with your Presence here.
Perhaps in your most Long and Glorious Reign
That other long and far less glorious rain
Was a deterrent – and I'm not surprised!
Yet tonight it is the Feast of Swithian.
And gentlemen in England – now abed —
Shall think themselves accursed they were not here,
And hold their manhoods cheap whiles any speaks
That were with us upon Saint Swithin's Day!
Our play for this, our Golden Jubilee,
Dark Lady of the Sonnets, doth depict
The meeting 'twixt the Bard and Good Queen Bess.
So while Elizabeth the Second sits
To watch Elizabeth the First, we pray
You gently to hear, kindly to judge
Our Play.

I delivered this prologue on the night at the Open Air Theatre – a night so chill and wet that we all needed warming
afterwards.

As any member of AA will tell you, the first drink is the most
dangerous and that bottle of claret set me off on more and more
bouts. 'Bouting' was my particular brand of alcoholism. As I've
already mentioned, I could go for long periods without drink
while I was working but then something – the end of a run or,
as at Scarborough, the need to get down to a daunting task –
would set me off. Vodka was my usual tipple, though when
I was in the throes I wasn't too choosy. I might get through
a bottle and a half at a go. Anyway, that particular bout
culminated in November 1983 in my appearance before the
magistrates at Bow Street accused of being drunk in charge of
a motor vehicle.

I had got myself severely pissed at a Red Cross charity event

150

and had then parked before calling at the CAA (Concert Artists' Association) to delivery some toys for their Christmas bazaar. Pam Cundell, an old friend from Fol-de-Rol days, had tried to dissuade me from adjourning to an Italian restaurant, but I went, and poured yet more down me. I then climbed into the car, went to switch on, and was promptly climbed on by two police officers.

I was under arrest and, having observed that one of the officers was Chinese, I don't think I advanced my cause all that much by telling him gravely that I wasn't playing Wishee Washee that Christmas. After cautioning me in the usual way they suggested I accompany them to Bow Street. When the case came up the next morning a charming lady barrister pleaded my cause with skill, but I still got a hefty fine and was banned for nine months. The news of my fall from grace made considerably fewer headlines than the front-page splash of a few years later, by which time, ironically, I was taking steps to get to grips with the problem.

At home we have spare bedrooms for our children should they – heaven forfend – all decide at the same time that they've had enough of what life has to offer and want to come home to Mum and Dad. It's a sort of haven in Avon. Despite the pain my alcoholism caused, we have always been an immensely close, loving family. The accommodation also doubles up as suites of rooms on happy occasions such as our silver and ruby wedding anniversaries, Christmas and summer holidays.

In 1983, just before my appearance before the magistrates, Caroline arrived home to stay with the children – Sarah aged nearly five and Cathleen who was just three. It was a stay which was to last nearly two and a half years.

Caroline's marriage to Philip Lynott, the lead singer in the group Thin Lizzy, was in trouble. Poor Philip was in the grip of a disease similar to mine, except that in his case it was drugs. It is our one regret that we never got to know our son-in-law better. We nearly made it on one happy occasion when Caro and the girls were staying with us while Philip was busy in town writing. He came down to Bath for the weekend and I met him off the train. He looked so alone and defenceless, standing on the platform with a great bunch of flowers. Caroline and the girls were enormously pleased to see him.

But eventually the disease caught up with him. It was Christmas Day 1985, and we were in the middle of lunch when Caroline received the news that he had been taken desperately ill at his house in Kew. She left immediately, collected him and took him first of all to Clouds House, the alcohol and drug dependency centre in Wiltshire to which I too went for help some three years later. But Philip was too ill for their help, and at their suggestion Caroline rushed him to Salisbury Hospital where he died in the Intensive Care Unit on 4 January 1986. His funeral took place at the beautiful Church of the Assumption at Howth near Dublin, and I was honoured by being asked to read a passage from Ecclesiastes 3, verses 1–11:

> There is a season for everything, a time for every
>   occupation under heaven.
> A time for giving birth
> A time for dying
> A time for planting
> A time for uprooting what has been planted
> A time for killing
> A time for healing
> A time for knocking down
> A time for building
> A time for tears
> A time for laughter
> A time for mourning
> A time for dancing. . . .

After my reading we sang 'The Lord of the Dance', which they had sung at their wedding. But it was the priest who took the service who paid Philip the greatest compliment when he described him as 'the father of Irish rock'. He was also the father of Sarah and Cathleen, whom we had been glad to look after with our daughter Caroline at our home for two and a half years – welcomed the chance, indeed, since it was some form of atonement for our never having completely understood him.

But even after Philip's sad death it still didn't enter my thick skull that I was in the same addictional boat as he had been. Realisation didn't come until I went to Clouds House, the one place which might have given life to Philip, and which gave life to me – renewed life.

Come on Down!

One of my great happinesses at this period was my new home, it has been ever since. The views from both the front and back of the house have alone proved worth the move. From our front door we look across the Avon valley to Kelston Tump – the full stop at the end of the Cotswolds – and from the back gate to Newton Park and down to the church tower and roofs of the village. In the winter months the curls of smoke from the chimneys and the early morning mist make ghostly silhouettes of the houses nestling in the dip below: a memorable sight.

Memorable also, and a measure of the passing weeks, is the sound of the bellringers practising each Friday evening. Every 23 September they gather in the belfry of All Saints and prepare to ring 'Fritz's Birthday Peal'. Having done so, they rest from their exertions, lift their glasses of cider or the like and give a toast: 'Happy birthday, Fritz!' Fritz Bartelt had lived in our house – indeed it was he who in 1909, when he was about to get married, converted the old farmhouse, Prospect House, into its present guise as an Italianate villa. He served as an officer in the Somerset Light Infantry in the First World War and died in 1916, aged twenty-nine, while serving in India.

Fritz was a churchwarden of All Saints, and in his memory his mother had a new set of bells struck, each of which bears his name. She also left a sum in perpetuity for a memorial peal to be rung annually on 23 September, his birthday.

Fritz's widow and two small sons had left the house and village soon after his death. One of the sons, Peter Bartelt, now an elderly gentleman, heard me on the radio one day in a programme called *The View from My Window*. He wrote me a nice letter saying that he had been born in the house and how pleased he was to hear how much we loved it

Having just heard the story of Fritz's birthday peal, I rang Peter and mentioned it to him. To my amazeent he said he knew nothing of this ceremony, so in 1984 we invited him to stay with us that September. On the 23rd he went down with us to the church and heard his father's peal for the first time – though not the last, as he has been several times since. It was wonderful. I think he was quite affected by the ceremony – just as I am when I think of the villagers gathering in the church to pray for me after my accident.

By gum, they are a mixture when you see them gathered in the village shop-cum-post office run by John Wright, like me a cricket nut and inevitably known as Arkwright – though sadly lacking a district nurse in the shape of Lynda Baron. My daily trip down the lane to collect the post and a paper and to mull over England's performance, wherever they may be playing, is always a pleasure – and one which I can now indulge more often.

The village is full of characters. Mind, when you have an ex-postmistress named Cynthia Payne it really is a scriptwriter's dream! When the case of the notorious Madame Cyn and her house of pleasure came to court and was splashed in all the headlines I teased our Cynthia unmercifully. Luckily at that time it was simply a post office – John added the shop when he took over – so I couldn't supplement my bawdiness with illustrative cucumbers and the like.

I once introduced our local admiral to a visitor with the facetious remark: 'This is our village admiral: every village should have one.' It provoked the immediate response from the admiral: 'Yes – and every village should have a comedian: we're still looking for ours.'

St Teresa's nursing home for the elderly – once the family home of the Bartelts, where Fritz grew up – is an important feature of the village. Jean's mother lived there for the last three years of her life and was lovingly tended by the nuns. They are a wonderful group of people with a direct and honest approach to life. Charlotte's wedding on 9 August 1986 was blessed with glorious weather and one day soon afterwards, in

156

the post office, Jean was gloating to one of the sisters about how lucky we'd been. 'Ah, well,' she said, putting Jean firmly in her place: 'The Divil's own get the Divil's luck' – by which it will be gathered that some of the nuns are of Irish descent. They are staunch followers of everything, both religious and temporal, that the village gets involved in, turning up regularly to support the annual Crowther plant sale in aid of church funds and always attending our pre-Christmas concert in the church given by the Laetare Singers, with recitations and readings to which I love to contribute. After one Christmas Jean asked the Mother Superior if they'd had a good time. 'Oh, 'twas grand,' she replied. 'Nobody died!'

In 1981 the celebrations for the Prince of Wales's wedding were held in the village street. They followed a sports afternoon on the playing field which had ended with a tug-of-war, St Teresa's *v.* the village (the anchor man for one of the teams was dressed as a nun). St Teresa's won. There was, of course, a tea party and a special cake was presented to the oldest inhabitant – a resident at St Teresa's, of course. It left her slightly bewildered, but you would be at over a hundred, wouldn't you? We had less luck finding seven vestal virgins to dance: no sooner had seven been mustered than one let the side down! The day ended at Church Farm, where we danced the night away.

Our village hall has been the scene of many a social gathering. The village Olympics took place there – the *Crackerjack* book of games was very helpful – and our Victorian and French evenings have been great successes. A monthly market is still held there under the expert supervision of churchwarden Bette Parfrey and her team of village ladies. All the money goes towards refurbishing the church.

Sadly I had to miss one occasion, held to mark the departure of two stalwarts of the village, John and Lily Harrill, who were going to live at Frome in Somerset. Derek Richards, the organiser, had asked me to say a few words, but as I was absent working the lot fell to Jean. 'Write me something,' she said, whereupon I recalled an occasion on which Lily and I had very nearly crossed swords – in fact we *had* crossed swords. I decided to immortalise this event in ersatz Victorian doggerel of the Robert Service variety, and here it is:

FAREWELL TO JOHN AND LILY

It was Sunday night in the Barton,
A night they speak of still,
A night they name as the night of shame,
When Les called Lily 'Lil'.

It seems no one had told our Les,
And that's something he can't forgive,
That no one in Corston called Lily 'Lil'.
Not if they wanted to live.

He hadn't been living there long himself,
As he sauntered down the hill,
At the Harrills' house he saw John's spouse
And he called out 'Wotcha, Lil?'

Her eyes grew wild, her bosom heaved,
She cried out, 'Don't you start,
'I was named after a flower, me lad,
'And not a Klondike tart.'

It was weeks before she forgave him,
But now they're the best of friends,
He even called her Lilian once,
In an effort to make amends.

Now some might think it's silly,
But whenever our Les walks by
The house where John and Lily
Used to live he starts to sigh.

He remembers the warmth of their welcome,
The day he first came here with Jean,
He remembers their work for the village,
And the towers of strength they have been.

And yet in that welter of memories,
The spectre that haunts him still,
Is the night that he came down the Barton,
The night he called Lily 'Lil'.

158

It went down like a bomb, Jean told me, and Lily was crying with laughter – how I wish I'd been there to see it.

In 1984 the Doldrum Years in my working life came to an end when I entered what William G. Stewart described as the Big League. Bill was the producer of *The Price Is Right*, the American show which took British TV by the scruff of the neck and firmly shook it.

Like most good game shows, *The Price Is Right* was mathematical in its precision and pace. I had to learn to describe briefly, clearly and accurately twenty-five different games, which were chopped and changed around to give each show variety. The audience comprised nine coachloads of people who arrived at Central Television's Studios in Nottingham from all over the country. As they queued up to enter the studio each one was given a sticker on which his or her name would be written, with a number to stick below it.

Once they were seated in the studio Bill Stewart, who had been a Butlin's Redcoat in his youth, would perambulate through the audience and proceed to chat them up. What he was looking for was a mixture of characters – white, black, yellow, spinsters, widowers, dolly birds and gigglers from whom he could pick four men and five women to Come on Down into contestants' row. There they had to guess the price of a given object without exceeding its true price. The person who was nearest to its actual price then joined me on stage to play a more complicated game for a larger prize, and from there he or she would either be eliminated or placed on hold for the sixfold finale. As a space became vacant in contestants' row I'd call the name of someone else to Come on Down. When we got to six in the finale we'd whittle it down to two grand finalists who had to compete for a showcase – always a breathtaking selection of prizes.

As Bill proceeded through the audience he would talk to them, mentioning names. He had previously worked out a coded message with his secretary, and she would know which ones he wanted on stage. She would then relay the numbers to the cameramen so that they could be lined up and ready when the moment arrived.

The names were written on cards and handed to me as the show started, and at that time the audience would be asked to remove their numbers. Naturally each coachload was hoping that one of their party would be chosen. In this way you got marvellous audience participation – they loved it when someone they knew was in contestants' row, asking them quite blatantly the price of an article, or whether they should keep or discard a prize. The noise of an entire coachload of voices yelling advice was hard to describe – people would also write signs in the air as a prompt – and they were usually wrong! Never before had a studio audience behaved with so complete a lack of inhibition – it was like a pantomime. And never before had there been so wonderful a selection of prizes.

The studio recordings were going magnificently and I was loving it. Then lightning struck: there was a technicians' strike at the studio and everything ground to a halt. Everything, that is, except the coachloads of potential participants, who like so many Sorcerer's Apprentices kept on arriving at the studio. I entertained them (I hope) with my cabaret act, for which a piano was brought in. Fortunately at the time the strike struck we had recorded four shows – a month's worth – so provided things could be settled fairly quickly the viewing public need never know.

Jean and I had booked to go on our first holiday to Canada and the USA and were supposed to be leaving on 16 April, by which time all the recordings should have been completed. As the strike was still on, Billy Marsh, who was now my agent, suggested we go ahead but leave him contact numbers in case he needed to call us back. The first show went out on Saturday, 14 April, and the press hated it with a vengeance. Too American, too loud, too full of greed – the notices were vitriolic. But the reaction of the public was staggering. When we arrived at London Airport on the Monday to leave for Canada and the States, cries of 'Come on Down' echoed all around and we were given royal treatment.

We had been away for almost two weeks of our month's holiday when, the night before we were due to fly to Los Angeles, the telephone rang. It was Billy Marsh telling us that

(a) the strike had been resolved and (b) *The Price Is Right* was number one in the ratings. 'So Come on Home!'

We flew to LA the next day and spent Friday with Louise Alexander, a noted antiques dealer and good friend of ours. She took us to the airport on the Saturday to fly home. Handsomely, Central Television came up with first-class tickets – the first time we had flown in such luxury. One of our travelling companions was the golfer Nick Faldo, whom everyone was congratulating. Apparently he'd won a major title in the States, but we'd been in such a rush that we hadn't found out what it was, so our felicitations were a bit inhibited.

Back at home it was down to more recordings of *The Price Is Right*, which kept its place in the ratings and looked set for a long run. Bill's prediction that it would propel me into the Big League proved absolutely right. Shop openings and other lucrative personal appearances came thick and fast.

Then, as so often in showbusiness, a black cloud appeared on the horizon – this time it came from Blackpool. Billy Marsh and I had arranged to put on a stage version of *The Price Is Right* at the Opera House in the summer of 1985, and I was to receive what seemed to be a generous percentage of the takings once the overheads had been covered. I felt certain I was on to a good thing, but when the time arrived for the first payment I encountered Billy with head in hands – never a good sign. He explained that the prizes – which were quite valuable – were always being won, something that we hadn't accounted for.

I reacted with incredulity. 'What? Do you mean that I'm going to be working for nothing all season?' Ruefully, he confirmed that such was the probability. There was no consolation in the knowledge that Bill himself would be losing a packet on the deal, because he's the sort who keeps his word and pays out if he's promised to do so.

We were sadly let down by Blackpool. Innocently, we had devised three variations of the show with three sets of prizes and three different levels of prices, but the show-going citizens had worked out that it was possible, by handing three sets of cribs to those attending a particular show, to ensure dead cert winners. And so it went. No matter how much I tried to giggle deceptively, the audience regularly deprived me of my salary by coming up every time with the right answer.

Fortunately, however, the television version kept going, and indeed it even became a favourite with some of the Yuppies. At one recording a party of them turned up in the studio and Bill chose one of them to 'Come on Down'. The young man, who worked in the City, was bright and on the ball and he cleaned up, knowing the price of everything. Afterwards he wrote to Bill saying that he and his friends would like to run a *Price Is Right* ball, the money raised to go to any charity we cared to nominate. At the time Jean was president of Abbeyfield, a charity for the elderly, in Keynsham, who were trying to buy a house to turn into sheltered accommodation. So we agreed and went along to the evening, which was great fun – the top prize was a Reliant Robin! Afterwards we were able to give Abbeyfield a nice cheque.

Then in May 1988 a reporter called at the house and told me he'd heard that Central TV were going to drop the show, asking if I had any comment. That was the first I'd heard of it – and to this day Central TV have never contacted me or offered a word of explanation, so I still don't know why.

It had been lovely while it lasted, but by far the most dangerous consequence of it ending – apart that is from cutting off my lucrative earning capacity! – was that it allowed my incurable disease to regain its hold on me. I hadn't been drinking all the time I'd been doing *The Price Is Right*, but the minute the discipline of all that was relaxed the drink took over again.

A Life Anew

The evil thing about alcoholism is that it sneaks up on you when you least expect it. It's just sitting on your shoulder, waiting for you to make that first slip. Of course the newspapers predictably put it down to my disappointment at being sacked from *The Price Is Right* but as usual they got it wrong. The truth is it's a disease and ultimately incurable. The best you can do is to keep it at bay and *never* lower your guard.

As I remind myself constantly, I achieved my rock bottom in alcoholism, my nadir in drinking, my slough of despond, in the autumn of 1988. My memory of that time is, of necessity, hazy. But the orgy of drinking which preceded it is deeply engraved on my mind. So are the many excuses I used for staying at our London flat where I could drink to excess the hooch with which I'd loaded the car. I would even hit the vodka bottle *en route*, half-bottling it while pulled off the road. I must have been mad.

On my rock-bottom morning in late October, at home in Avon, I waited until Jean had left the house to attend to the flowers in church, then did my usual tour of inspection of the decanters until I got quite hazy – even though I knew I had to open a fete in Glastonbury that afternoon. With the misplaced confidence of the alcoholic I had no doubts that I could cope with it all, but when Jean returned and challenged me with being drunk I realised that I could no longer go on pretending, and asked for help. I even needed help getting my trousers on! She filled me up with black coffee and said she would drive me to Glastonbury. I was in no condition to argue.

The gentleman organising the fete was waiting for us in a

pub where I'd arranged to meet him, and of course he offered me a drink – which I declined with some lame excuse. What followed was dreadful – I can't remember what I said, but I know that never before had I uttered such balderdash before an audience. I did a quick tour of the stalls and left early, with Jean supporting me all the way.

On the way back home I started to cry, and I cried all evening. The following day I at last got in touch with the Alcoholics Advice Bureau. Meanwhile my children had taken the law into their own hands. Adam – Charlotte's husband – rang someone he knew who was a counsellor at Clouds House, the alcohol and drugs dependency centre. He actually fixed a date for me to go there and was unbelievably firm with me – made me pack my pyjamas and toothbrush, razor and towel. It was like being packed off to boarding school.

Tim, the counsellor, met us in the hall at Clouds and Adam waited while he cross-examined me. I didn't know it, but I'd already taken the first of the Twelve Steps of the AA creed – I'd admitted that I was powerless over alcohol and that my life had become unmanageable. I was accepted into the inner sanctum and it was there that I first met Peter Pugh, fabulous Welshman, devout cricketer, and counsellor. I knew there was something special about the man the moment I clapped eyes on him, and so it proved.

Peter acted as MC for group therapy, during which we 'peers' discussed our mutual problem. I uttered the customary self-introduction: 'My name's Leslie and I'm an alcoholic', and the rest of the group welcomed me with a 'Hi, Leslie', which was also a sign that they believed me.

The awful truths I learned about myself from those plain-speaking, non-theatrical folk! But I had another problem – small compared with the one which had brought me to Clouds, but important to me. As I explained to Peter, I was under contract to appear in pantomime in Bath in five weeks' time, and felt obliged to honour it (I've always been quite adamant that a contract is a contract – part of my ingrained professionalism, I suppose).

'All right,' said Peter. 'If we let you go, do you promise you'll come back?'

'You have my word,' I replied, we shook hands on it, and I've never touched a drink since.

Jean collected me next morning but, sadly, no sooner had I left than my alcoholism hit the headlines, making the front page of the *Sun* and, the following day, the *Daily Mirror*. A fellow patient who couldn't take the toughness of the course had walked out of Clouds and, needing money, had sold the story of my presence there to the *Sun*. The paper admitted as much, whilst declaring their intention to keep the identity of their informant a secret to protect his name! What about *my* name, I thought, splattered in four-inch print all over their front page? But I gritted my teeth and faced life.

Then something horrible happened. Jean and I were in London to see my agent, and in the evening had been to see a wonderful Mike Leigh film. We were walking up St Martin's Lane to get a taxi and were passing the entrance of Stringfellows, the night club, when one of the waiting paparazzi spotted me and shouted out my name for all his fellows to hear.

Like a pack of hounds they were round us. 'I don't want any photographs taken,' I said, hailing a cab which thankfully pulled up. As we were entering, a photographer pushed in and pulled the window down, allowing them all to get their loathsome cameras in and take flash shots. I then climbed out. This was the worst thing I could have done, since one of them immediately straddled the back of the taxi with his body, with the obvious intention of making up a story that there'd been a fight. Realising this quickly enough, I got back into the cab and we drove on to the flat.

I swear it was that which brought on my heart trouble. I lay awake half the night, burned up with the indignity of it all.

First thing the following morning my agent, who was now Billy Marsh's associate Jan Kennedy, rang me and said, 'City Desk have been on the phone with the message that several staff reporters have filed stories that you were drunk in St Martin's Lane last night.'

'Well, they're lying,' I said, to which she replied, 'I've already told them that.' I've never trusted reporters or cameramen since.

Anyway, we duly opened in Bath in *Robinson Crusoe* – new to me unless you count the New Cross Empire production all those years ago with Dorothy Squires, so I was naturally somewhat nervous. What with that and the somewhat ungracious publicity I had received I felt it judicious to keep a low profile in Bath, let alone in my own village.

In my drinking days such a nightmare episode would have driven me to the bottle – but not now. If anything it strengthened my resolve never to drink again. And all was not lost: pantomime at Christmastime is a rare dispeller of gloom, and I flung myself into it wholeheartedly. We were blessed with a wonderful cast: Janet Dibley played Crusoe, Chris Harris Mrs Crusoe and Glyn Owen the Captain. They all treated me superbly – not a mention of my alcoholism. We opened to thundering good notices, and the panto ran till the end of January.

I then had to gird my loins for the return to Clouds – though this time I looked upon it not as a chore but as an opportunity to grasp the nettle and make myself alcohol-free. I'd had my first taste of the sober world and couldn't wait to consolidate my gain.

I knew already that I was a 'bouter' and that I would need all the ammunition I could muster to fight the disease. The AA provided essential support through its programme of total self-honesty. There were no distractions at Clouds such as TV, radio, books or newspapers – no family visits, even, except on occasional Sundays. You rose at seven and you went to bed, once you'd finished your homework, at midnight.

The regime involved a lot of straight talk from peers, an awful lot of humility from me, and a terrific amount of TDs (Therapeutic Duties to you – not DTs as one of the peers insisted it should be called!) There was a lot of sense in TDs. They trained you to involve yourself in real life instead of just concentrating on drinking or whatever your chosen addiction was. The training was almost hypnotic, weaning you off even the thought of having a drink. At least that was my experience. By far the worst TD was the Big Wash – washing up twenty-eight plates, cups and dishes – a never-ending task as pile after pile of gubbins stared you in the face. No sooner

166

had you apparently cleared the decks than you got another lot delivered by the table monitor.

Next to the Big Wash in its horrendousness as a TD was what I called the Wakey-Wakey routine. Armed with a brass bell you made the alarm-call noise in all the corridors, waking up the sleeping peers. It didn't make you desperately popular, I can tell you!

Being on belling duty meant you'd be woken from your slumbers by a nurse thrusting the bell into your defenceless hands as an indication that your tour of duty had arrived. Undue humour was frowned upon. Thus the Liverpudlian who rang his confounded bell outside my room and yelled out, 'Leslie Crowther – Come on Down' was immediately deprived of it. I was similarly lucky when I supplemented my bell-ringing with the cry: 'Unclean, unclean!' and 'Bring out your dead!'

The hoovering and dusting I really enjoyed, but what made Jean fall about with laughter was the fact that we had to do our own laundry – shirts, smalls, everything. It was easy to tell those who lived alone: they sailed through it. But for the rest of us who were spoilt by other halves it was torture! I still hate ironing.

The AA creed is a spiritual one, based on admitting that there is a power greater than oneself. The programme has twelve steps for you to work through, and at Clouds they helped you with the first five.

Step one   We admitted that we were powerless over alcohol and that our lives had become unmanageable. I'd taken this step when I went for help to Clouds, but to make the step afully conscious one first I had to write out my life story – and then write truthfully about how my dependency on alcohol had affected various areas of my life. This is some of the writing I did in February 1989, from which you will judge what a painful exercise it is.

Family Life
1. I am obsessively tidy, and like everything to be in its

167

proper place. I know this gets up Jean's nose, especially when I put a book back in its allotted place in the bookcase that she had just taken out to read! Tidying up the house after a party, or when guests have gone, or even when the grown-up children or grandchildren are there, is another total obsession. Yet when I've had a drink (as I thought secretly) I couldn't care less.

2. Effects of my drinking on Jean have been so numerous over the years that it's a wonder she hasn't left me. She has in fact given me two serious ultimatums, both written, and I have gone dry for a while on each occasion and then lapsed again. Lying to her on the telephone when she has asked me if I was drunk because my speech was slurred, and my insistent denial that I'd had nothing to drink at all. Secret drinking in the house – especially over the last six years – and hiding bottles all over the place. Coming home two hours later than I had promised after a cabaret engagement, very pissed, and Jean sitting white-faced with anxiety in bed. This has happened often from 1965 onwards.

3. When daughter Charlotte deputised for Jean at a charity ball I had promised to attend in 1979 – Jean was otherwise engaged – she was very excited because it was her first ball. We sat on the top table with Lord Delfont and other theatrical heavyweights, and I gradually had too much to drink. Although I danced with Charlotte, conducted the charity raffle, and thought I was being very sociable, the proud father became ashamed during the evening because I knew my senses were dulled. I didn't stagger about or disgrace myself, but Charlotte knew the difference between sober and alcohol-affected Dad. On the way back she was very quiet and tense as I was concentrating hard on driving safely. I despised myself all the way home.

4. Many times when the children were growing up, I missed out on sharing their education and their young lives, because I was so preoccupied with alcohol. The times I can remember, and there are not enough examples, are very precious to me. I wasn't pissed all the time of

course, but I had drink on my mind. With the eldest girls it wasn't so bad, because they were seven by the time I was going into television, and the drinking problems slowly began. But with Caroline, Charlotte and Nick, I missed out on a hell of a lot.

5. We moved to Bath in 1978, and I was really trying to control my drinking. Nicholas was twelve, Charlotte fifteen, Caroline nineteen, and the twins were twenty-three. The girls certainly were aware of my problem. Morally I have always wanted to set a good example to my children, and in certain areas I think I have. A stable marriage, professional approach to work, belief in God, caring for others, charitably minded, a good home-maker. Yet time and time again I have let them down by being an alcoholic. Alcohol has made me actually dislike Jean intensely, when she wouldn't let me get away with my 'little problem', as I liked to think of it. On many occasions, especially in the sixties and seventies, we would lie on our backs in bed frozen with resentment, neither giving way, and neither prepared to make the first move towards making peace with the other. I hated those nights, and half the time I really couldn't see that it was all my fault. Or as I know now, the actions caused by my illness. And I love her more than anyone or anything on this earth.

Powerlessness
Powerlessness over alcohol is the first thing an alcoholic must admit to, and *accept*, if he is to even begin recovery. I realise now that even one drink will open the floodgates, and lead to disaster and death.

The powerful hold alcohol has over an alcoholic is so great that it makes it impossible for him to control the amount he drinks. More sinister than that, it always gets progressively worse. The powerlessness gets greater and accelerates. That has certainly happened to me. My periods of abstinence were getting shorter and more infrequent, and the increase in the amount consumed more and more. It had begun to take a complete hold of me, and I – on my own – was powerless to prevent it.

My powerlessness was becoming complete – indeed had always *been* complete – and I was just beginning to recognise it. That powerlessness in an addict is born with him, and will eventually kill him unless he does something about it.

Unmanageability

An alcoholic may appear to be managing his life, but in reality never does, because he is planning that life, wittingly or subconsciously, around the next drink. I was able to manage that side of it, I thought, so far as work was concerned, for years. Thinking about it now, I can remember several occasions when I did a bad job the day after a hard session, and twice being almost incoherent; once on stage and once in cabaret. An inability to face writing letters or making important telephone calls has manifested itself recently. Of course one's personal life is incredibly affected, because every lie and deceit is invariably detected.

> **Step two** We came to believe that a power greater than ourselves could restore us to sanity.

This step is primarily an attitude change and once again required more writing and discussion in groups with other patients. They could quickly see through me when I tried to duck an issue – just as I could see through them when they did the same.

> **Step three** We made a decision to turn our will and our lives over to the care of God as we understood Him.

In 1981, whilst in Scarborough with *The Black and White Minstrel Show*, Jean and I had been confirmed together in a lovely little church on the moors. I had attended church in Twickenham and then in the village we moved to whenever I was free. This step really required me to 'Let Go and Let

God'. This certainly seemed to have been the case when I appeared on breakfast television and HTV on the Friday evening following the week of headlines and cartoons in the *Sun*. I publicly stated my willingness to become sober. I was not seeking publicity for me, but I was trying to ensure that the public knew my feelings about the potential harm to the aim of AA that the media attention was causing. Certainly a Higher Power gave me the courage and the right words and saw me through.

Step four   We made a searching and fearless moral inventory of ourselves.

This is the most painful part of the whole course, writing it all out truthfully and honestly.

Step five   We admitted to God, to ourselves and to another human being the exact nature of our wrongs.

Having worked hard through these steps, now I had to read everything I had written to a listener – someone who came in from AA – a terrifying ordeal which took three hours. Luckily my listener was a very pleasant and kindly man who instilled in me no fear at all. I did this the day before I left Clouds House.

There were two instances at Clouds when I nearly threw in the sponge. They were a test of my resolve from God. I found a hateful article referring to me in *Today* on the second Saturday that I was there, and I also had a panic attack when HTV were allowed to come in and film a visit from the Duchess of York. Some patients never did see the course through. They found it all too painful an exercise and walked out. Thank God, I managed to complete it.

Of course there were some lighter moments – one came one Friday evening before I left when I performed a couple of parodies I'd written to entertain my peers. One was a song from *Oliver* by Lionel Bart:

171

Booze, glorious booze
Makes me feel so flustered
When we start to use
Our brains turn to custard
First think of the life we led
Just not caring
Now we are alive not dead
Now we are sharing.

Life, glorious life
Good usually conquers
Let's give up the strife
Or we'll all go bonkers!

When I left Clouds, after a stay of only six weeks, Jean, the family and myself were all delighted. Especially me, because with no drinks bill I was in pocket!

I was looking forward to practising those five steps and the other seven, hopefully for the rest of my life. Jean came to collect me on 17 March 1989. We drove home across country, through an assortment of villages and landscapes which were all new to me, and a strange feeling of contentment fell upon me – a contentment which has lasted, thank God, until the present day.

Whenever I go back to Clouds House with Jean for reunions – which take place three times a year – it is always with a sense of awe. There in that funny old house with its atrium and its nicotine-stained drawing room ceiling you find yourself one of a gathering of four or five hundred people, sharing their delight in new lives. An amazing sound fills the crowded corridors, bringing back floods of memories: the sound of laughter and joy, of relief from the agony of despair: 'Amazing Grace, how sweet the sound that saves a wretch like me-me-me: I once was lost but now I'm found: was blind but now I see. . . .'

Now I only think about drink in meetings of AA when we openly discuss our former problems. I actually look forward to those meetings, because it does you good to remind yourself of what you've come through and to meet others who are just starting out, experiencing the same problem. An alcoholic is the only person who can lie in the gutter and look down on the rest of the world!

But work – that was the immediate problem. Who would employ an ex-alky with lowered self-csteem? Well, luckily I was a firm favourite with Christine Williams, the producer of *Crosswits* on Tyne Tees TV, and she invited me to do a week's guesting on the programme. There was little else, apart from a series of Allied Carpets store openings, which I enjoyed, and a few cabaret dates.

So in my spare time I started a new career as Master Builder, kicking off with Operation Tree House. Our eldest grandchildren and their parents had moved to a house in Batheaston which had a garden running down to the river, and at the end of the garden was a large willow which was crying out for a tree house.

I worked out my plans carefully, bought the materials from a DIY shop in Keynsham and bore them to Batheaston in the Rolls, planks garlanded with a red flag protruding from an open window – a silly sight. But there was nothing silly about the tree house – it was a great success. I even thought of slapping a preservation order Grade I, House, Tree Variety, on it.

But it was while working on the tree house that I started to get very breathless. I took myself off to my quack and it was then that my heart irregularity was diagnosed. He sent me to see a heart specialist at the Bath Clinic who carried out the usual tests. After a break for what proved to be my last pantomime – in Croydon – I returned to the Clinic in January 1990, now with a strangulated hernia. This, of course, required surgery, but as the surgeon's name was Robin Smith – namesake of the England No. 3 batsman – I knew I was halfway to recovery before the operation had started.

After recuperation from that, something fabulous happened: two ministering angels from TV came along with a programme called *Stars in Their Eyes*. Jane McNaught, who had been a production secretary on *The Price Is Right*, had gone into production on her own and was tied up with Granada TV and Dianne Nelms who was chief of Light Entertainment there under David Liddiment.

The programme had originated in Holland, and in March

1990 Jane, Dianne and I flew over to see it being recorded. We all loved it, and it was decided to go into production here. But first, the girls decided, my image had to be brushed up – or rather down. They invited Jan Kennedy, now my agent, and me to dinner at L'Escargot in Soho on a snowy night in 1990 and there, over a gourmet meal which was to set them back a hefty three-figure sum, they proceeded to discuss me entirely in the third person, as if I were elsewhere.

They concentrated first on my hair, which they considered both too sloppy and over-brilliantined. I didn't mind that so much, but when the 'decision' was reached to divest me of my glasses I came out of my snail-shell to utter a mild protest.

'I'll have a fairly complicated autocue to read,' I pointed out, 'and I've never used one before. There'll be yards of script and I just don't see myself getting through it blind – unless you can get it produced in Braille.'

The three of them (Jan now seemed to be on the side of the angels) looked at me pityingly before reaching the unilateral decision: *contact lenses!* And that is what I wore.

I couldn't help thinking, as our two lady hostesses picked up the tab, that it was an expensive way of smoothing my hair and removing my specs. In fact I remarked as much to Jan as we trudged through the deep snow to the tube station, all road traffic having been immobilised: 'It seems a hell of a price to pay for the privilege of telling me that my image over the last few years has been bollocks.' I daresay similar thoughts were stirring in the handsome heads of Jane and Dianne, and what these two high flyers thought as people came up to me in the underground for autographs or simply to say 'hello' I've often wondered.

An odd occasion. But never mind: Sarah, my eldest grand-daughter, made it all worthwhile after she'd seen the first transmission: 'She rang and said 'groovy hairstyle, Grandpa.'

The show went into production, and the first programme was transmitted on Granada TV in July 1991. Happily it found favour with the viewers, and *Stars in Their Eyes* was a success. I had made three series before my accident and will never forget those marvellous performers, for some of whom it was their first time in a TV studio. My job was to make them feel at home – a job which was made easy by the production team: Jane and Dianne, who looked after them all like a couple of mother hens, and Chris Power, the choreographer, who was like a brother.

Another 'brother' figure was Ray Monk, among other things the musical director – the principal 'other' being passionate cricket lover. During one run of rehearsals there was cricket on the rival BBC channels for six hours a day. Ray and I discovered a set in the rest room for scene assistants on which we could watch the noble game, and on frequent occasions we were missing from the set of *Stars in Their Eyes*. When discovered, we would sidle back in sheepishly, but Jane of course took it all in her stride.

Among the many multi-talented guests I reckon that the best three – and incidentally the three series winners – were Maxine Barrie, who was a fabulous Shirley Bassey; Bernard Wenton, a great impersonator of Nat King Cole; and Amanda Normansell, a Welsh schoolgirl who was a brilliant Patsy Kline. There was an amazing contrast between the contestants when they were being themselves and when they had taken on the personalities of the stars they were emulating. Their natural nervousness when interviewed out of character had totally disappeared by the time they walked through those famous doors as the living images of those whom they were shadowing. The team of make-up artists, too, deserved a lot of credit for the physical transformations – but the amazing thing is that the contestants sounded even better than they looked. What excitement, and how simple an idea – but then, like most good ideas, its simplicity was the secret of its success.

The Noble Game

Those readers who have got this far may have detected a leaning towards the ancient and noble game of cricket, though I must at once make clear that, although a keen player since boyhood, I have seldom distinguished myself on the field of play. Indeed, my cricketing skills were aptly summed up by the remark of a Bathonian spectator at a Lord's Taverners match on the Bath CCC ground. Positioned at deep square leg I was vainly trying to stop balls from the bat of Farokh Engineer, the star Pakistani wicket-keeper and ferocious batsman, sailing over the boundary when a voice from the crowd called out: 'I've seen you moving faster in Sainsbury's'.

But both the game of cricket and its players have been one of my chief delights. I've been extraordinarily lucky in the friendships I have made with some of cricket's great names – a number of which I first encountered during the Scarborough Fol-de-Rol days.

From 1961 to 1966 I was a member of the Black and White Minstrels' cricket team, a force to be reckoned with in its heyday, with victories chalked up against police and army elevens and other worthy opponents. Now and then we were able to reinforce the side with professionals from the Yorkshire County Club – thanks to the Scarborough connection – and on one occasion, against an army team, had secured the services of Don Wilson and Philip Sharpe. Both were Test players – Don a left-arm off-break bowler and Philip an opening batsman of renown – who for some obscure reason were being 'rested' from the Yorkshire first eleven. For some reason Don took against a particular member of the army eleven, a rather snooty chap, and the upshot was that he bowled him five balls in one over

177

that he just couldn't lay his bat on, then clean-bowled him with the sixth. The batsman in question was suitably mollified afterwards when Don came clean about his identity.

On another occasion Tom Sloane, who was not only chairman of the Kew Green CC but also head of BBC Light Entertainment, asked me to provide some cricketers of note to reinforce the team in a charity match for Kew Green CC – they would be wearing disguises contrived by a BBC TV make-up team. It was a Sunday match and, as there was no Sunday League cricket in those days, my Yorkshire friends agreed to turn out. And turn out they did, to great effect.

The match took place on the village green, adjacent to which was a pub with a garden running down to the Thames. The pub manager got severely pissed before the batting opened and promised to pay the charity £50 for every six hit over the pub roof and into the river. At this the under-cover Yorkshiremen's eyes sparkled and ball after ball sailed over the roof to splash into the Thames. Johnny Hampshire even pulled a six on to the upper deck of a 90b bus, which presumably took it on to Mortlake Crematorium. At the end of the innings the charity was in benefit to the tune of £450.

Matches such as these brought me ever closer to the realisation of my ambition to become a Lord's Taverner, which I achieved early in the swinging sixties, becoming member no. 577. Two framed posters dating from around that time, advertising charity matches sponsored by Rothman's of Pall Mall, hang proudly in our downstairs cloakroom. One is for Colin Cowdrey's XI v. Leslie Crowther's XI, the other for the Lord's Taverners XI v. Leslie Crowther's XI.

The Lord's Taverners club was founded over forty years ago by a group of actors, broadcasters and musicians who loved the game and watched it whenever they could from the Old Tavern at Lord's Cricket Ground. They decided that, as they all had professional and sporting interests in common, it would be a good idea to start a club, based at their beloved old tavern, where they could talk about their work and watch cricket and 'try to put a few bob back into the game at the same time'. The first task was to appoint a suitably prestigious captain, and by dint of pulling strings at Buckingham Palace an interview with Prince Philip was obtained. A useful cricketer in his own right, the Prince readily agreed to take on the job and it was eventually agreed that he should be styled 'Patron and Twelfth Man' – which he still is, over forty years on.

The club was a success from the start and has certainly raised a few bob – many millions of pounds, in fact. Since 1987 the annual sum raised has exceeded £1 million, all of which has been donated to organisations complying with the charity's main objective – to provide facilities for young people to play sports of all kinds and thus keep them off the streets and away from the associated risks. The principal means of raising funds has been to stage cricket matches between teams of celebrities from theatre, film, TV, radio and the various sports. These have always been hugely popular. As there was no Sunday League cricket at the time of the club's inauguration people turned up in considerable numbers for the Taverners' Sunday matches, and even today they still do so.

I can still see the late Graham Hill haring towards the boundary chasing a ball which he had no chance of overtaking without the benefit of four wheels. And I can hear that great Kent wicket-keeper Godfrey Evans shouting: 'For Gawd's sake keep 'em up a bit' to J.P.R. Williams, the famous rugby international – who must have found handling a spherical ball a bit novel. On the sidelines, faithful supporters manned the autograph tables where those 'names' who weren't actually on the field of play would be busily signing autographs and raising money. Volunteers also manned booths where you could have your photograph taken with the star of your choice.

Some of the celebrities went round with a blanket, inviting spectators to fling in loose change. On one occasion we collected £400, more than enough to buy a new set of tyres for a New Horizon mini-bus. These, incidentally, are specially equipped mini-coaches which the Lord's Taverners provide at minimal cost to youth organisations, particularly for those involved with disabled people.

The commentators on the BBC's *Test Match Special* would often give a plug to the Sunday charity matches, which was very much appreciated, though Fred Trueman's description of my bowling was somewhat unkind, if accurate: 'Leslie

Crowther, slow left arm, something terrible.' My fielding probably merited a similar put-down, especially in my later years. On one occasion in a match played at Brympton D'Evercy in Somerset, a defensive push from the opposition's opening batsman prompted me to indulge in a fake exhibition of fielding skill. It went horribly wrong and I split the webbing between thumb and forefinger. At Yeovil Hospital where I went for minor repairs the Irish medico in the accident unit muttered as he stitched me up: 'And you say we Irish are bloody mad.'

Mad or not, I returned gamely to the field of play where Leslie Thomas, the captain of the Taverners XI, welcomed me with: 'Thank God you've come back – you're in next.'

'What do you mean "in"?' I replied. 'I'm due at a cabaret engagement tonight and I'm playing the piano.' (I fulfilled the engagement, albeit bandaged up.)

I ended up taking a turn at the microphone to do a spot of commentary, and was just in time to witness an amply-proportioned female pal of Jilly Cooper's take off all her clothes and do a streak round the wicket, to the amusement of all present. In a moment of heaven-sent inspiration I was able to add to the general mirth by recalling an old music hall joke which I trotted out over the air: 'I don't know what she's wearing, but my God it doesn't half need ironing.'

These days I just act as umpire.

In 1984 Jean and I took a decision which was greatly to enhance our enjoyment of the noble game and life in general. When we sold our Twickenham house we had retained an upstairs flat for use whenever we were in London. Having moved to the West Country, we soon found this inconvenient. Paddington was now our London railway terminal and it was quite a way from there to Twickenham. So we decided to sell the flat and look for another near Paddington, preferably near to Lord's (we wanted jam on it!).

We got it, too. The flat we found was in a block called Lord's View One and we went for it like a shot. I mean, anything with the name 'Lord's' in it had to be worth the price, and as we'd just embarked on the second series of *The Price Is Right* it was right in more senses than one. The flat is on the upper floor of the block, with a balcony overlooking the hallowed sward and the grandstands. Oh, those grandstands! They are structural and architectural gems, particularly the Mound Stand. But they are a mixed blessing to some, of course, such as the occupants of the flats overlooking them – including us!

When we moved into the flat we could see the entire ground, including the boundary rope on our side. I mentioned our glorious view to Fred Titmus one day during the early part of the 1986 season, and he nearly fell apart with laughter. 'You haven't seen the plans, then?' he managed to get out when he'd finished wiping his eyes. 'I should sell now and cut your losses, if I were you.'

I took no notice at the time, but later in the year we were watching a one-day final from our balcony, with the telly on just inside the door so that we could dive in and watch the live action replay, when Jean's mother rang up.

'He's on telly!' she screamed excitedly to Jean, who'd answered the phone.

Equally excited, with images of repeat fees forming in my mind, I yelled back: 'Well, what is it? *Black and White Minstrel Show*, *My Good Woman*, *Whose Baby*, or what?'

Jean relayed the message back.

'No, you fool,' she said. 'You're on, live, now.' I leaned inside the room to watch telly and did the Harry Worth one arm and one leg in the shop window bit. I saw myself doing it on the box. As I was wondering what to do next to amuse the viewing millions I heard the voice of Tony Lewis. He was laughing in the same way Fred Titmus had done. 'He'd better make the most of it while he's still got the chance,' he chortled.

Only then did we realise that the imminent rebuilding of the Mound stand would cut out our view of the pitch, leaving us only our present uninterrupted view of the Grandstand scoreboard and anyone fielding at long leg or deep third man. The plans had been nailed to the wall across the road for months but I'd ignored them. Never mind: the stand adds greatly to the comfort of those watching the cricket, and we can still see them practising in the nets!

181

In July 1990 I had the first intimation that I might be on the point of realising my ultimate cricketing ambition – the presidency of the Lord's Taverners. Tim Rice was approaching the end of his third year as President – unusually, as a two-year term is the norm – and it was in a letter from him that I received the hint: 'It was at a recent meeting of the Council that I asked the question: "Who is going to succeed me as President?" Their response was: "The President will emerge." Well – for better or worse, you are emerging.' I wrote back to say how pleased I was to be an emerging President, and in due course I broke out of my shell into the most fulfilling two years of my life.

Tim had been a highly successful President in every way – hence his extended term of office. It was going to be a hard act to follow, but I resolved then and there to put maximum effort into maintaining the high standards that he and the rest of the Taverners team had set, though I was aware that the recession, along whose bottom we were still bumping, would make money-raising an even more daunting task than usual.

Fortunately I would have Jean at my side. From the start she was as keen as I was to make it a success. I won't say she's as crazy about cricket as I am (I can think of few people who are), but she's always had energy to spare and is a born organiser, being one of the few who can organise me.

I like to think that we didn't do too badly. At least our Patron and Twelfth Man was kind enough to commend my efforts towards the end of my two-year stint, and he is not noted for calling a spade a garden facilitator! Here is the letter which formed the title page of the November 1992 issue of *The Long Room*; the journal of the Lord's Taverners which was printed for the Annual Ball.

It has never been a good time to raise money for charity, only some times are worse than others. 1992 has been one of the latter, but, thanks to the tireless activities of the President and the success of the annual Ball, there is every chance that the Taverners will reach their target for the year.

To give you some idea how much we owe to Leslie Crowther, I have calculated that if he had been given

10 pounds for every mile he has travelled on Lord's Taverners business and a thousand for each of the events he has attended, this Ball would only need to raise fifty thousand pounds to reach the target of one million. As it is, he wasn't and the target for the Ball is a good bit higher, but I am sure that people will be as generous as possible so that none of the beneficiaries of its charity will suffer.

How delighted he must have been – as were I and all the Taverners – when his youngest son 'emerged' to take over from me at the end of my presidency. Prince Edward is proving to be a most successful President, and I shall always remember his kindness in visiting me in Frenchay Hospital after my accident.

The President's year always starts with the Umpires' Dinner, which is a meeting of ex-presidents and likely lads to whom the incumbent can turn in the unlikely event of a last-minute let-down. The year then fills up with charity cricket matches and other events. Of the latter, one of the most rewarding is the annual concourse of New Horizon mini-coaches provided and equipped by the Taverners. In May 1991 the first of what we hope will become an annual jamboree was held at Chessington World of Adventure, when forty vehicles full of handicapped boys and girls were entertained by the Lady Taverners – an association of women who are interested in cricket and who have become a highly successful and glamorous splinter group of the Lord's Taverners. On this occasion it was their maternal instincts which lent so much heart to the occasion.

Another of the high spots of my presidency was the Eve of Test Dinner at the London Hilton in 1992. We were honouring Brian Johnston in his eightieth year, and our other principal guests were Nawaz Sherif, Prime Minister of Pakistan, and our own Prime Minister John Major – one on my left and one on my right. I saw fit to introduce them as follows: 'Gentlemen, you see before you two for the price of one. Now I don't mind the attendant MI5 Security: I don't even mind the fellow crouched between my legs. It's just the strange feeling I get in the spot where he rests his Kalashnikov: every time he shifts he makes me an offer I can't refuse. . . .' There then came the extraordinary moment when Nawaz Sherif said he would like Pakistan to give our great charity some money – he bore a cheque and asked if we thought £50,000 would be all right. It was quite unexpected generosity. John Major retorted that he'd like to do the same, but he'd never get it past Norman Lamont.

The highlight of the evening came with the presentation to Brian Johnston of a specially inscribed cricket bat. In making the presentation on behalf of the Lord's Taverners John Major invited a 'very special guest' to hand it to him. Brian turned round and there was his wife, Pauline, who had been especially smuggled into this all-gentlemen's evening for the occasion. Missing Brian, as we all do, it is some consolation that we were able to honour him thus towards the end of his long and distinguished service to the game he loved.

As the term of my presidency was drawing to a close Jean and I went to Northern Ireland with a team of Taverners. It turned out to be a most successful visit, during which we formed the nucleus of a Northern Irish branch of the club. The hospitality we enjoyed there was second to none and we received repeated thanks for making the journey despite all the adverse media coverage Northern Ireland received.

Then it was back to England to prepare for the five functions which remained before the President's Ball, which would be the culmination of my two years in the hot seat. After that I was booked to record another series of *Stars in Their Eyes*. I promised myself that after my sixtieth birthday the following year Jean and I would take life more easily – the last two years (and indeed my entire life, in retrospect) could scarcely have been harder!

We were to receive a sad blow on 30 September – Jean's mother's death. Poor old darling, she had enjoyed a long and very good innings, but the working parts were not working any more. For the past three years she had been looked after by the dedicated nuns of St Teresa's nursing home in the village, and visited almost daily by Jean as the devoted daughter on the spot. The nuns were among the large congregation present at her funeral on Tuesday, 6 October. But by then I, too, was lying at death's door in Frenchay Hospital, with more than a likelihood of filling the same role in the same church! I suppose if I'd been conscious I'd have reflected that attending a Lord's Taverners function in Swansea followed by the opening of two Allied Carpet stores and then travelling home had been asking for trouble. I might even have wryly reminded myself of the old adage: 'Death is nature's way of telling you to slow down.'

The Day I
Officially Went Grey

No sound effects department could re-create the noise I remember as the Rolls hit the central reservation of the M5 and cartwheeled over and over towards the verge before coming to rest upside down.

Although pretty shaken up, I realised I had to get out. For one thing it felt as though I'd broken my neck: consequently I felt as if I were being throttled. Gingerly I went about the unharnessing of my safety belt and worked my way through the open window on the driver's side to discover a lone figure staring at me. It was grinning – with relief as much as anything, I would think.

Eventually, although I've no idea now of the timescale, an ambulance and a police car arrived – I can't remember in which order – and I was able to tell first one and then the other the home phone number and – miracle upon miracle – which tablets I was taking for my heart. I also asked the one question which I suppose hits all AAs – had I been drinking? I also wondered if anybody else had been involved. The police assured me that neither seemed to be the case. Still *compos mentis* I was taken to Cheltenham hospital where I remember being told that Jean had phoned and said she loved me. There being nothing else on my mind, I lost consciousness.

I woke up I don't know how much later in Ward 2 at Frenchay, sprouting tubes from every conceivable orifice, so much so that I started to remove the most available ones – the ones up my nose – since they got up my nose figuratively, too. This caused grief to my nurses, who anchored my hands, but I defeated them. It's a wonder they didn't ram the tubes right back with the force I deserved.

The nightmares started then: little insignificant nightmares, but bad dreams just the same. I dreamed that Ward 2 was built on to the side of our house, connecting to Sarah and Cathleen's bedroom and/or to Charley and Adam's, and I couldn't wait to get back home again and discover that everything was just as it had been.

When, months later, I had well and truly recovered from the accident and was back home there was nothing, apart from the short-term memory loss, to remind me that I had so recently been on the brink of death.

I tried to remind myself of it all, but all I felt was sheer horror and disbelief at what had happened. It was only after seeing all that had been written about the accident and its aftermath in the press, and reading all the lovely cards from well-wishers and the letters from friends – or being approached by strangers in the street who all expressed delight at my recovery – that I finally accepted that it had indeed all happened.

Someone asked me recently how I thought the accident has affected me. 'Deeply,' I said to them, and to myself I said it's taught me the difference between despair and hope.

Despair was when I was totally unable to remember words, or started a sentence which I found I couldn't complete. I had gone through so much only to find myself speechless as if I had dried up on stage. I knew what I wanted to say but couldn't get it out. I'd use a quick visit to the loo – on the pretence that the tablets were working (sometimes they were!) to have a few minutes in solitary to get my fuddled memory in place, emerging with the words and phrase on my lips.

Hope was provided by the speech therapists at Frenchay, Rachel and Jacqui. They forced my muddled brain to work again, and recently tested me by setting me a target to learn a poem called 'Timothy Winters'. The poet is Charles Causley and I strongly recommend anyone who hasn't made Mr Causley's acquaintance to see to it that they do so.

Why me? I asked myself when I was near to death. I can only think I was called back to make amends to my family and especially to Jean. It is the AA's Eighth Step – become willing to make amends with them all.

Since the accident I have learned through my grandchildren how important my children are.

The best present when I came out of Clouds in 1989 were twin grandsons, children to my eldest daughter Lindsay and her husband Peter. They live in Hastings, rather too far to commute, but the entire family come and visit in the holidays and make good use of the swimming pool (when it's hot!). The twins are identical as can be and are called Anthony and Matthew. They are brothers to Sara and Kristina and they are blessed with loving parents Peter and Lindsay. Pete is an interior decorator who helps us out in our house. Consequently it never or hardly ever looks scruffy. Peter is a highly methodical worker, and sooner than let a place be, he worries about it until it's perfect. I think some of the pernicketyness has rubbed off on Lindsay. Lindsay is exactly the same with motherhood.

Liz, her twin, is unmarried and lives in Twickenham, in one of the finest flats that have been the source of our family furniture that you could wish to see. She has appeared on TV programmes like *Shoestring, Munsfield Park, The Bill* and is currently appearing in Alan Ayckbourn's latest production *Communicating Doors*. She is a fine actress, and we're both very proud of her. Not only that, but we relish her company.

Caroline is married, or rather remarried, to a charming chap called David Taraskevics which is a surname you have to gird your loins and take a flying leap at. Half Latvian, half Austrian, and in the musical business. David spends his time mounting rock concerts. They have four children ranging from a beautiful brunette named Sarah, Phil Lynott's daughter aged fifteen, to a macho son Luka, aged one. In between comes another of Phil Lynott's girls, who has incidentally inherited her father's true singing voice, one Cathleen, and another of the Taraskevics, Natasha, a beautiful blonde, four going on forty! Luckily they all live near us

Charlotte and Adam only live in Corsham, just a few more miles away, and have delivered us of Alexander who has a thing about dinosaurs, and can draw them accurately, and Clemency who has the voice of a fishwife and does not live up to her name.

189

Whether or not she has inherited her voice from Charlotte I am not prepared to say, but I do know that Alexander has quite definitely inherited his drawing skills from Adam, who is a successful trompe l'oeil artist, operating all over the country. And in our house, strangely enough! All it wants is for me to learn carpentry, and we'll be quids in!

Caroline and Charlotte have each attached themselves to a drama group, Caroline being a very funny performer, and Charlotte being a kindly but determined director. And we *all* know where that comes from: Granny and Grandpa!

Nick has followed them both in professional terms, having a career in broadcasting – he now reads the AA Road Watch for S.E. England. He is also the proud holder of a First Class Honours Degree in Fine Arts which he gained at Newcastle-upon-Tyne University. But there is little or nothing work wise for a First Class Hons. Bachelor in Fine Arts, so Nick has gritted his teeth and became a waiter in L'Escargot, as well as having a much more satisfying career in broadcasting. His wife Claire, having survived a career as 'Red Claire' in socialist circles and sat outside no. 10 and no. 11 Downing Street more times than I could mention, has presented Nick with a redhead (typical!) called Leah, and a not-so-redhead called Sacha.

This June I even kissed Fergie, yet another redhead otherwise known as HRH the Duchess of York, fourt times at the British Institute for Brain Injured Children – which boosted my recovery no end.

I've made good progress in the past eighteen months – thanks to Jean, the rest of the family, friends and all the wonderful care and support of the specialists and staff at Frenchay. I discarded the zimmer some months ago, relearned to swim the crawl and play the piano – and of course learned the new skill of autobiography!

I've also had heaps of opportunity to say a heart-felt thank-you to all the people who've stopped me in the street or met me at cricket matches to tell me how well I look.

But even so I think the first time I realised how ill I'd been was when I saw the recording that someone had made of my handling of the press outside Buckingham Palace after the investiture. I couldn't help noticing how frail and sparkless I'd become. Now the one thing an actor needs in pursuit of his or her career is energy. Without that it is impossible to achieve the sort of professionalism which is owed to those who do you the privilege of paying their hard-earned money to come and see you. Consequently, much as I would love to carry on in my chosen profession, I have decided to retire. My thoughts can be summed up in a poem by John Betjeman called 'The Last Laugh':

> I made hay while the sun shone and my work sold.
> Now that the harvest is over and the weather grows cold
> Give me the bonus of laughter
> As I lose hold.

I think I really reached this decision in Frenchay on the day when my hairdresser, Richard, had just finished cutting my hair and asked if I wanted to continue dying it. I toyed with the idea, looked in the mirror, decided I looked *très distingué*, and gave the idea the big E.

So Charlotte, you've got your answer to that question you asked me years ago when I'd been driving you I don't know where, and with my hair dyed a particularly virulent shade of sheep-dip: 'Daddy – when are you officially going to go grey?'

Index

Index

193